746.4   Taylor, Gertrude   75-396
T   America's crochet book.

	DATE DUE		
Mar 27 '75	May 10 '76		
Apr 11 '75	May 26	Jan 17 '78	
Jun 27 '75	Aug 27 '76	Feb 2 '78	
Sep 11 '75	Sep 8 '76		
Oct 13 '75	Nov 23 '76	Aug 8 '78	
Oct 20 '75	Jan 10 '77	Jan 17 '79	
Dec 1 '75	Feb 19 '77	Jul 11 '79	
Dec 22 '75	May 24 '77	Oct 24 '79	
Feb 3 '76	Jun 20 '77		
2-20 '76	Nov 16 '77		
Mar 9 '76	Dec 12 '77		

AMERICA'S
CROCHET BOOK

AMERICA'S CROCHET BOOK

Gertrude Taylor

Illustrated by Cathy Goodale
Photographs by Saul Pliuskonis

Charles Scribner's Sons/New York

TO ALL THE NIMBLE FINGERS,
past, present, and future

3 5 7 9 11 13 15 17 19 MD/C 20 18 16 14 12 10 8 6 4 2

Printed in the United States of America
Library of Congress Catalog Card Number 72-1209
SBN 684-12976-0

Acknowledgements

Without the help of good friends who brought me antique crochet pattern books dating back to the 1800s, some of the old stitches and trims would not have been included. My thanks are due to the following:

Ardath Browning, Mrs. A. F. Rewinkel, Betty Simmons, Harriet Saunders, Betty List, Jinx McDonald, Nora Koerner, Betty Knaus, Eugenia Hahnewald, and Wilma Slater.

Wilma Slater, while on a tour to Japan, purchased several Japanese crochet pattern books that proved to be a source of superb ideas for the chapter on medallions.

For assistance in making swatches, I wish to thank Connie Felts, Jinx McDonald, Harriet Saunders, Helen Campbell, and Sammy Cummings.

Also, I wish to thank
Sue Sivers for typing and proofreading
Mike Kirby for English correction
Cathy Goodale for illustrations
Saul Pliuskonis for photographs

The pattern directions which have been quoted in this book have come from several sources:

1. Patterns which have been handed down from generation to generation.
2. Pattern books which have long been out of copyright.
3. Patterns which have been made up by the author to approximate directions which would be found in most pattern books.

Contents

AMERICA'S
CROCHET BOOK

Introduction

If you would like to have a pleasant, rewarding hobby, you should try crocheting. You can satisfy a creative urge and gain great satisfaction by completing an unusual outfit that you could not buy in any store. All around you, people are busy with hook and yarn or thread, creating beautiful garments or useful articles for the home. Many people crochet just to have lovely garments, while others take up the art to have a relaxing pastime or a hobby. No previous sewing skill is needed—you can learn to crochet even if you have never done any other handwork. Crocheting requires techniques not used in other skills. You can learn these techniques! Your work can be carried around with you, so while you are lunching or waiting in front of the school to pick up the children, taking a coffee break at home, or resting between household chores, you can work a row or two. You will be surprised how much progress can be made by working a row here and a row there. Before you know it, one piece is completed and you will be anxious to start the next piece.

Crocheting, however, is a complicated subject. Don't let me discourage you, but you will need to do some planning in advance if your hours of labor are to produce the wanted results. So many people think that they need only to purchase yarn, hooks, and a pattern book to create gorgeous garments. This is not so. You must develop a new skill and start at the bottom of the ladder and move up rung by rung. If you have crocheted for years, making doilies, edgings, or tablecloths, you have a little head start on the brand-new beginner, but still you must learn how to fit, block, and finish garments made of yarn. There are so many, many poor, amateurish looking crochet gar-

1

ments being worn. It is regrettable that people who have obvious talent turn out garments that look homemade. I have seen ever so many poorly fitted and poorly finished garments that would be improved by better fitting and finishing techniques.

You will be able to do good work if you start out at your level. I know there are many beautiful patterns available now, and there is a great temptation to make coats and dresses before you have had sufficient groundwork. These will all come in due time. In the meantime you can be building your wardrobe with simple, small crochet pieces, which you will find interesting and useful. Your knowledge and skills will be developing and you can build on these skills. If you should jump into the midst of a hard project without sufficient background, you will find that you cannot fan out in every direction and pick up procedures which you should have learned previously. Learn the basic techniques first. Build on them. Learn the next step, and so on.

Learn to fit properly. You must learn how to take measurements and learn how much allowance is needed at the key places on the measurement charts that you will make. Any garment you intend to make will need careful planning and preparation before you start. This may take a little more time, but a garment well planned and carefully checked as you proceed will block to the exact measurements. It will then go together easily and can be finished beautifully. When you are finished, the garment will fit to your satisfaction. That will be your reward! Most people do not bother to do this extra bit of work, but if you do, you will be assured of a perfect-fitting garment every time. All commercial patterns must be adjusted to *your* personal measurements. These fitting problems will be discussed at length in the text.

1 Teaching Yourself to Crochet

General
If you are left-handed
Types of hooks and hook sizes
Steel hooks
Aluminum or plastic hooks
Wood hooks
Afghan hooks

Description of Beginning Stitches
Chain stitch
Extra tips for the beginner
Single crochet stitch
Extra tips for the beginner
Half double crochet
Extra tips for the beginner
Double crochet
Treble crochet
Double treble crochet
Triple treble crochet
Slip stitch

Shaping of Crochet Pieces
Decreases
Decrease in single crochet
Decrease in half double crochet
Decrease in double crochet
Decrease in treble crochet
Decrease in double treble crochet
Decrease in triple treble crochet
Increases
Bind off

Practice Stitches with Yarn
Joining new thread

1 Teaching Yourself to Crochet

GENERAL

If you are a beginner learning to crochet, you must learn how to handle the hook and how to form many of the lovely, simple stitches. Beginners can handle a fairly small hook and coarse crochet thread easier than they can handle yarn and a large hook. Yarn splits easily and the stitches formed from large hooks are quite large, resulting in holes which are not distinct. Because large hooks are awkward for a beginner to handle, you should use a number 1 steel hook and number 5 pearl cotton for learning to crochet and for working swatches. You must train yourself to watch and see everything that is going on—what you are doing and what causes it. You must see how the various stitches are formed. You must examine your work constantly so that errors can be detected and corrected. Practice on a sample swatch. Know the right side from the wrong side and know how the stitches look on each side. You must learn the abbreviations used in pattern books and a whole new vocabulary of crochet terms. For example, when the term "yarn over" is used, this refers to *either* yarn or thread. Pattern books are not instruction books. The pattern makers assume that you know how to work the many details that they require. You must learn to read and understand these pattern books.

All of this practice work before starting a project will pay big dividends. This is all fun and challenging work. This is your groundwork, and when all of these techniques are mastered, you can start a project. Then you can use yarns and larger hooks. If you have the desire to crochet well, you can do so. Take it slow and easy until you get the feel of crocheting, and don't be discouraged if you feel you are not working fast enough. Often a speedy crocheter's work is sloppy and uneven. After you have passed the initial period of struggle, you will be delighted with yourself, and speed will be acquired gradually. If others can do it, you can do it too!

If You Are Left-Handed

Left-handed people *can* and *should* learn to crochet right-handed. Hold the hook as right-handed people do.

Learn to hold your hook in your right hand, and with the thread over your left index finger as explained on page 8. Now you must learn to manipulate your right hand. It can be done with practice. Your right hand will hold the hook somewhat rigidly, however, your left hand will help a great deal. Hold your hook by perching your right hand on top of the hook through the finger grip depression (the flattened section). You will be surprised at how well your right hand can learn to work. In playing the piano or typing, one must learn to use both hands. You too can learn to do this. Undoubtedly most violin and guitar players are right-handed, yet all of the fingering is done with the left hand. The only duty of the right hand is to push the bow or to strum. If musicians can learn to use their left hand for fingering, you can learn to use your right hand for crocheting. If you do not learn to do this, you will be working from the opposite direction, and numerous problems will arise as you learn more of the difficult stitches. You must not work in the wrong direction because no one else can help you. All brand-new, right-handed crocheters are awkward in handling the hook and thread. They too must go through an initial period of struggle. Try! Practice!

Types of Hooks and Hook Sizes
Crochet hooks are grouped into four separate groups.

STEEL HOOKS
Steel crochet hooks range from size 00 (the largest) through size 14 (the smallest) and are five inches long.

00	used for knitting worsted-weight yarns or heavy cotton crochet threads
0–1	excellent for sport yarns and medium-weight cotton crochet threads
2–5	used for fingering yarns and lightweight cotton crochet threads
6–14	used for fine and very fine cotton crochet threads

ALUMINUM OR PLASTIC HOOKS
Sizes in aluminum hooks range from size E (the smallest) through K (the largest). Plastic hooks range from size D through Q. Most of these hooks are five and one-half or six inches long. The plastic size Q hook is eight inches long.

These hooks are used for varying weights of wool, cotton, or synthetic yarns.

WOOD HOOKS
The size range in wood hooks is 10 (the smallest), 13, 14, and 15 (the largest). They are nine inches long and are used for extra heavy yarns (or several strands of yarn) or for heavy cotton rug yarns.

AFGHAN HOOKS
Afghan hooks are made of aluminum or plastic and they are lettered the same way as regular aluminum or plastic hooks (from

size F to K). They are available in nine-inch and fourteen-inch lengths. Afghan hooks do not have a finger grip depression (flattened section); they resemble a knitting needle that has a hook on one end instead of a point. They are used for afghan stitch—a stitch which requires all of the loops in the row to be retained on the hook. This is why they are uniform throughout the shank and longer than the regular crochet hook.

The hook sizes are slightly larger with each increasing size. As the hook becomes larger, the shank also becomes larger. Each hook, with the exception of the afghan hook and the wooden hook, has a depression (a flattened section) approximately midway on the shank.

DESCRIPTION OF BEGINNING STITCHES

Chain Stitch (ch st)
The foundation of most crochet is the chain stitch. In order to begin the chain stitch, first make a slip knot approximately four inches from the end of the thread. Do this by making a loop, then pull another loop through the first loop. The slip knot loop is attached to the hook as shown.

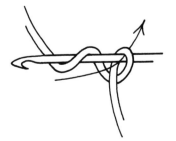

Notice the hand position. In crocheting, you must hold both your work and the loose thread in your left hand. Your right hand holds only the hook. You may use either of the two hand positions shown in the drawing. Hold the hook at the finger grip depression as you would a pencil or "perch" your fingers on top of the hook.

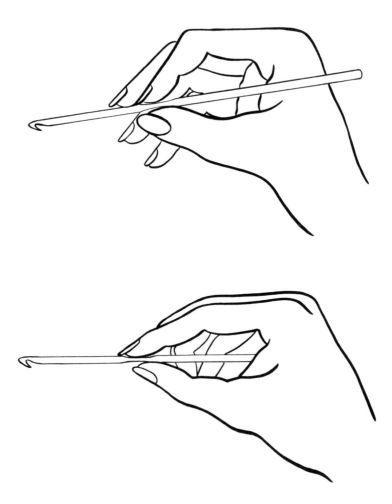

To work a long chain, hold the tag end of the thread remaining from your slip knot in your left hand between your *thumb and third finger*. Hold the thread coming from the ball of thread over your index finger. Try to get a little tug (tension) against the thread. Wind it around the little finger of your left hand before placing it over your index finger. With the hook in your right hand, lay the crochet hook in front of the new thread, wrap the thread over the hook, then, with the hook pointing down, pull a new loop through the loop on the hook. One chain stitch has now been worked. Continue making chain through chain for the desired number of chain stitches, or until you get the feel of doing the chain stitch.

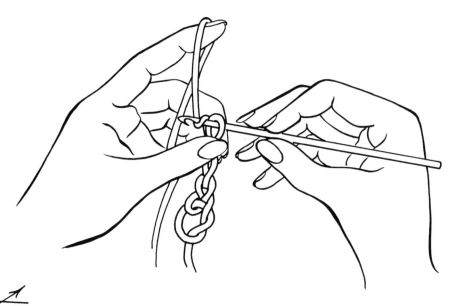

EXTRA TIPS FOR THE BEGINNER

1. You will find that you must keep raising the thumb and third finger of your left hand to hold the chain close to where you are working. In this way you will be able to pull the new stitch through the old stitch easily.

2. You will not be able to pull another chain through the old chain if you do not point your hook *down*.

3. Before you pull the new chain through the old chain, slip each new stitch completely onto the shank part of the hook to make all of your stitches the same size.

4: The chain you form must be flat. If it is not, you are not holding your hook in *front* of the loose thread and then bringing the thread over the hook. If your stitches are not flat, you cannot work into these stitches on the second row. Strive to make your stitches even. PRACTICE!

Single Crochet Stitch (sc)

Work a chain of twenty-one chain stitches as a foundation chain. Work on the foundation chain you just made as follows:

Step 1

    Sc in 2nd ch from hook and in each ch across.

In order to work into the second chain from the hook, count back on your work to the second chain from your hook. Do *not* count the loop on the hook as the first chain, Step 1. Now insert your hook into the chain, as shown in Step 2, placing the hook between the loops in the second chain so that *two* threads lie on top of the hook and one thread lies below the hook. Pull a loop through this hole. See Step 3. You now have two loops on the hook. Next, lay the hook in front of the thread, Step 4, yarn over the hook and pull a loop through both loops on the hook, Step 5. One single crochet stitch has been made. Work one single crochet stitch in each of the chains of your foundation row. Count back over the row of single crochet stitches that you have just made and you should have twenty single crochet stitches. Count as the

Step 2

Step 4

Step 3

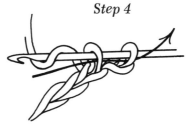

Step 5

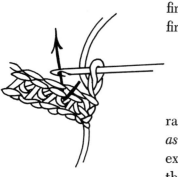

first stitch the little chain space you skipped when you made your first single crochet stitch in the second chain from the hook.

Work a second row of single crochet as follows:

Ch 1, turn, work 1 sc in each sc across row.

When you chain one and turn your work around, the chain one raises your work up to the level of the next row, and *it is counted as the first single crochet stitch.* Notice in the drawing that it is exactly on top of the last single crochet stitch that you made in the first row. Skip the next stitch and then single crochet in each stitch across the row, working through the top two loops of each single crochet stitch to the end of the row. Count again to make sure that you are maintaining twenty stitches and that you are counting your chain one at the beginning of the row as a stitch.

EXTRA TIPS FOR THE BEGINNER

1. Make sure that you are bringing each loop up onto the shank part of the crochet hook. In this way all stitches will be uniform and the work will not be too tight, which would make it difficult to work into the stitches on the next row.

2. Keep moving the thumb and the third finger of your left hand near to where you are working. You must also point your crochet hook down in order to pull the loops through.

3. After you have finished one row and are ready to start the second row, notice that you will be coming back over the row from the opposite direction.

4. When you turn your work around at the end of the row, you will see the *wrong* side of the stitches you made on the last row. You must become very "eye" minded. Notice how these stitches look as you are making them. On the next row, you must see how these same stitches look from the opposite side.

5. When working the second row, notice that the hole where you place your hook is just to the left of the stitch on the row that you have just finished.

6. Work back and forth on the twenty stitches for many rows. To begin the third row, chain one to raise to the level of the third row and *count the chain one as the first single crochet stitch.* Be sure to skip the first hole. If you do not skip this hole, you will have two stitches coming from the first stitch. Single crochet in the next stitch and in each stitch across the row, and work the twentieth stitch in the top of the turning chain of the previous row. Chain one and turn. Work all the following rows the same as the third row.

7. When you want to fasten off your work, work to the end of the row and cut the thread. Be sure to leave an end of approximately four inches. Pull the loose end through the loop on the hook to lock off the stitches.

8. If you have made errors in your work and want to rip out your work to correct them, simply take off the loop that is on the hook and pull out stitches until you have removed the errors. Then replace the loop on the hook and proceed from that point.

Sample of Single Crochet Stitch

Half Double Crochet (hdc)

Chain twenty-one stitches. Work across the chain, working through two threads as before:

> Work 1 hdc in the third ch from hook and in each ch across row, ch 2, turn.

To work a half double crochet stitch, you must hold your thread and hook as explained previously. That is, hold the hook in your right hand and have the thread coming from over the index finger of your left hand. Wrap the thread over the hook one time, Step 1, then place the hook into the third chain from the hook, Step 2, (do not count the stitch on the hook as one chain), and pull a loop through. You now have three loops on the hook, Step 3. Lay the hook in front of the loose thread, Step 4, yarn over, and pull another loop through all three of the loops on the hook, Step 5. One half double crochet stitch has just been

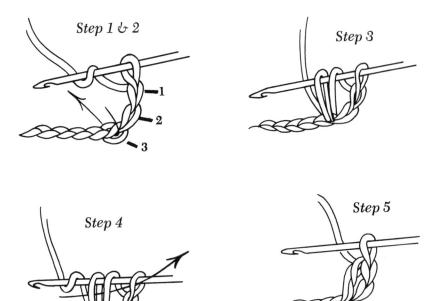

Step 1 & 2

Step 3

Step 4

Step 5

worked. Work one half double crochet stitch in each stitch across the chain. You should have twenty stitches, counting as a stitch the chain three at the beginning of the row. Chain two to count as the first half double crochet stitch for the next row.

On the next row, work half double crochet stitches in each stitch across the row. Maintain the count of twenty stitches.

EXTRA TIPS FOR THE BEGINNER

1. When you chain two to count as the first half double crochet stitch for the second row, it takes the place of the first stitch of the second row; therefore, you must skip the first hole. Then place your hook into the second hole as you did when you were working a row of single crochet stitches. The twentieth stitch should be placed in the turning chain of the previous row.

2. Work row after row of half double crochet stitches. Be sure that you are maintaining the twenty stitches for each row, counting the chain two at the beginning of the row as one half double crochet stitch.

Sample of Half Double Crochet Stitch

Double Crochet (dc)

Make a chain of twenty-two stitches. Work across the row, working through two threads of each chain as follows:

Work 1 dc in 4th ch from hook and in each ch across row, ch 3, turn.

Step 1 & 2

In order to work a double crochet stitch, hold your thread and hook as explained previously: that is, with the hook in your right hand and the thread coming from over the index finger of your left hand. Wrap the thread over the hook one time, Step 1, then place the hook into the fourth chain from the hook, Step 2 (do not count the stitch on the hook as one chain). Pull a loop through, Step 3. You now have three loops on the hook. Lay the hook in front of the loose thread, Step 4, yarn over, and pull another loop through two loops on the hook, Step 5. There are now two loops left on the hook. Yarn over and pull another loop through the last two loops on the hook, Step 6. One double crochet stitch has just been worked, Step 7. Work one double crochet stitch in each of the chains across the row. You should have twenty stitches, counting the chain four you skipped at the beginning of the row as one stitch. Chain three to count as the first double crochet stitch for the next row. Work a stitch in each stitch across the row. The twentieth stitch will be placed in the turning chain of the previous row. Maintain the count of twenty stitches.

Step 3, 4 & 5

Step 6

Step 7

Sample of Double Crochet Stitch

Treble Crochet (*tr or trc*)

Make a chain of twenty-three stitches. Work across the row as follows:

> Work 1 trc in 5th ch from hook, and in each ch across row, ch 4, turn.

In order to work a treble crochet stitch, hold your thread and hook as explained previously. Wrap the thread over the hook *two times*, then place the hook into the fifth chain from the hook, see drawing, Steps 1 and 2 (do not count the stitch on the hook as one chain), and pull a loop through. You now have four loops on the hook. Lay the hook in front of the loose thread; yarn over, and pull another loop through two loops; see Step 3 (three loops left on the hook), yarn over again, and pull another loop through the next two loops on the hook, Step 4 (two loops left on the hook); then, *yarn over and pull another loop through the last two*

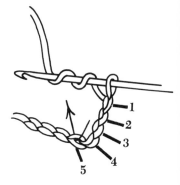

Step 1 & 2

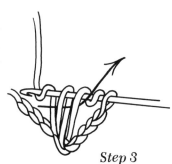

Step 3

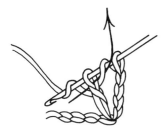

Step 4

Step 5

Step 6

loops on the hook, Step 5. One treble crochet stitch has been worked, Step 6. Work one treble crochet stitch in each chain across the row. You should have twenty treble crochet stitches, counting the chain five you skipped at the beginning of the row as the first treble crochet stitch. Chain four and turn your work around.

On the next row, work a treble crochet stitch in each stitch across the row. The chain four after turning counts as the first treble crochet stitch. The twentieth stitch should be worked in the top of the turning chain of the previous row. Maintain the count of twenty stitches. Work row after row of treble crochet stitches, constantly counting to make sure that you have not increased any stitches or decreased any stitches.

Note: When working the second row, after you have chained the four stitches to turn, notice that the chain four comes directly on top of the last treble crochet stitch you worked before you chained four and turned. Because you already have a stitch on top of the last stitch of the previous row, you will not put another stitch through this stitch. Put your next stitch on top of the second stitch of the previous row.

Sample of Treble Crochet Stitch

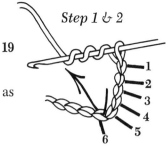

Step 1 & 2

Double Treble Crochet (*dtr*)

Make a chain of twenty-four stitches. Work across the row as follows:

> Work 1 dtr in the 6th ch from hook, and in each ch across row, ch 5, turn.

In order to work a double treble crochet stitch, hold your thread and hook as explained previously. Wrap the thread over the hook *three* times, Steps 1 and 2. Then insert the hook into the sixth chain from the hook (do not count the stitch on the hook as one chain), and pull a loop through. You now have five loops on the hook. Lay the hook in front of the loose thread, yarn over, and pull another loop through two loops, Steps 3 and 4 (four loops left on the hook). Yarn over and pull another loop through the next two loops on the hook, Step 5 (three loops left on the hook). Yarn over and pull another loop through the next two loops on the hook, Step 6 (two loops left on the hook). Then, yarn over and pull another loop through the last two loops on the hook, Step 7. One double treble crochet stitch has been worked, Step 8. Work one double treble crochet stitch in each chain across the row. You should have twenty double treble crochet stitches. Count the double treble crochet stitch in the sixth chain from the hook at the beginning of the row as the second double treble crochet stitch, and count the chains you skipped as the first double treble crochet stitch. Chain five and turn your work around.

On the next row, work a double treble crochet stitch in each stitch across the row. The chain four before turning your work

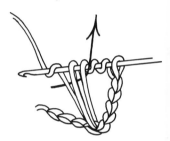

Step 3 & 4

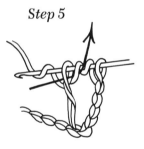

Step 5

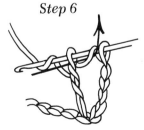

Step 6

Step 7

Step 8

Sample of Double Treble Crochet Stitch

around counts as the first double treble crochet stitch, and the twentieth stitch should be worked in the top of the turning chain of the previous row. Maintain the count of twenty stitches. Work row after row of double treble crochet stitches, constantly counting to make sure that you have not increased any stiches or decreased any stitches.

Note: When learning to work the double treble crochet stitch, bear in mind that you must wrap the thread over the hook three times before starting to work the loops off. Then, when working the stitches off two at a time, you will yarn over and pull a loop through two loops, yarn over and pull a loop through the next two loops, yarn over and pull a loop through the next two loops, and yarn over and pull a loop through the last two loops on the hook.

Triple Treble Crochet (*tr tr*)

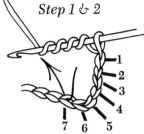

Step 1 & 2

A triple treble crochet stitch is worked in the same way as a double treble crochet stitch, except that you must wrap the thread once more over the hook before starting to work the loops off. You must wrap the thread over the hook four times. Place the hook in the seventh stitch from the hook, Steps 1 and 2. Then work off two loops at a time, five times, Steps 3, 4, 5, 6, and 7. One triple treble crochet stitch has been completed, Step 8.

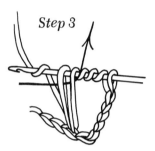

Step 3

Make a chain of twenty-five stitches. Work across the row as follows:

> Work 1 tr tr in the 7th ch from hook, and in each ch across row, ch 6, turn.

Note: Work a swatch of triple treble crochet stitches, maintaining the count of twenty stitches. See photograph of triple treble crochet stitches.

Step 4

Step 5

Step 6

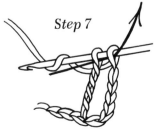

Step 7

Step 8

Sample of Triple Treble Crochet Stitch

Slip Stitch (*sl st*)

A slip stitch is a very small stitch. Make a foundation chain. Insert the hook into the second chain from the hook, Step 1, yarn over the hook, and pull a loop through the stitch and the loop on the hook, Step 2. One slip stitch has been worked, Step 3. Work a row of slip stitches across the foundation chain.

Note: other uses of the slip stitch: A slip stitch is used when joining, or when closing a chain for a picot stitch, or when some stitches are to be bound off. Your pattern will give you instructions on how to join or bind off.

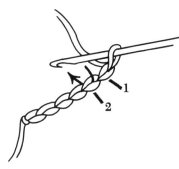

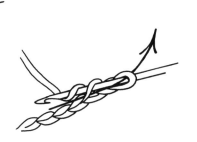

Step 1   *Step 2*   *Step 3*

SHAPING OF CROCHET PIECES

If you are going to make *anything* that is not a straight piece, such as a shell or a blouse, you must crochet your shaping as you proceed. If you want to make your piece wider, you must increase some stitches, or if you want to make your piece narrower, you must decrease some stitches. Your pattern will direct you to increase, decrease, or bind off. Learn to do this before you start your first project. Practice on one of your sample swatches.

Decreases

Decrease means to get rid of one stitch at a time. In order to decrease stitches, read the following instructions and practice on one of your sample swatches.

DECREASE IN SINGLE CROCHET

To decrease in single crochet, draw up a loop in each of the next two stitches, yarn over and draw a loop through all three loops on the hook. (See drawing.) One stitch has been made from two stitches. Examine your work. Below the closing of the stitches, you will be able to see the two stitches as one stitch. On the next row, when you are to work into the top of *this* decreased stitch, you will place only one stitch through this decreased stitch. Count the number of stitches across the row to make sure you are now maintaining the required number of stitches after decreasing. In many instances, your pattern directs you to decrease at the beginning and at the end of the row. You will work a decrease in the first two stitches and in the last two stitches.

DECREASE IN HALF DOUBLE CROCHET

To decrease in half double crochet, yarn over the hook, insert the hook into the first stitch, yarn over the hook again and insert the hook into the second stitch (five loops on the hook). Then, yarn over and pull a loop through all five loops on the hook.

DECREASE IN DOUBLE CROCHET

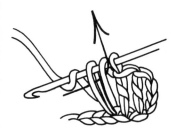

To decrease in double crochet, your pattern may read; "Hold back last loop on each of the next two double crochet stitches, yarn over hook and pull a loop through all three loops on hook." In doing this step by step, you will yarn over hook, insert hook into the first stitch, yarn over and pull up a loop, yarn over and pull a loop through two loops on the hook (two loops remaining on the hook), yarn over, insert hook into the second stitch, and pull up a loop, yarn over, pull a loop through two loops (three loops remaining on the hook), yarn over and pull a loop through all three loops on the hook. If you examine this decreased stitch, you will see that two stitches at the base of the stitches have been worked off as one stitch at the top of the stitches. Learn to see how these decreased stitches look after they have been worked off as one stitch.

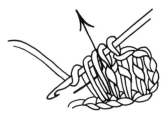

Step 1

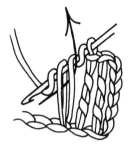

DECREASE IN TREBLE CROCHET

To work a decrease in treble crochet, hold back the last loop on each of the next two treble crochet stitches, yarn over and pull a loop through three loops on the hook. In doing this step by step, you will lay the yarn over the hook two times. Insert the hook into the first stitch, yarn over and pull up a loop, yarn over and pull a loop through two loops, Step 1; yarn over and pull another loop through two loops, Step 2 (two loops left on the hook). Start the next stitch with yarn over two times. Insert the hook into the second stitch and pull up a loop, yarn over and pull a loop through two loops, Step 3; yarn over and pull a loop through two loops, Step 4 (three loops left on the hook); yarn over and pull a loop through all three loops on the hook, Step 5. One decrease in treble crochet has been completed, Step 6.

Step 2

Step 3

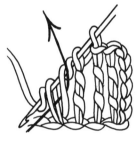

Step 4

Step 5

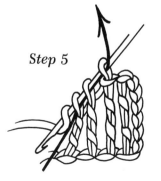

Step 6

DECREASE IN DOUBLE TREBLE CROCHET

To decrease in double treble crochet, work as instructed for a decrease in treble crochet. That is, hold back the last loop on each of the next two double treble crochet stitches (three loops left on the hook), yarn over and pull a loop through all three loops on the hook.

DECREASE IN TRIPLE TREBLE CROCHET

To decrease in triple treble crochet, work as you were instructed for a decrease in treble crochet. That is, hold back the last loop on each of the next two triple treble crochet stitches (three loops left on the hook), yarn over and pull a loop through all three loops on the hook. Do not do anything automatically. Examine your work carefully and you will see that two stitches have been taken off as one stitch. Count the number of stitches you have on the last row, making sure that you are obtaining the number required *after* decreasing.

Increases

It is a simple process to increase in any stitch. Simply place two stitches in the stitch where you are to increase. Place the two separate stitches through the hole where the one stitch was to be placed. Count the number of stitches after you have completed the row to make sure that you are maintaining the number of stitches required after increasing stitches.

Bind Off

If your pattern wants you to bind off some stitches, the pattern maker wants you to begin your next row several stitches in from the end of your piece of work and to end that row several stitches in from the other end of your work. When you are working on a garment and are shaping the pieces, and you must shape for the armholes, your pattern will ask, for example, that you bind off five stitches at the beginning and at the end of the row to start the armhole shaping. Some patterns do not give you step-by-step instructions to do this. It is assumed that you already know how. In order to bind off, you will need to slip stitch across the top of the next six stitches (which leaves five stitches unworked—the sixth stitch is the first stitch of the next row), then chain the number of stitches required for the type of stitch that you are working to raise your work to the level of the next row. You will then start the next row from that point (five stitches in from the edge) and work across the row until you approach the other end of the piece. At this point, you will leave five stitches unworked at the end of the row. This gives you a sharp "takeoff" on each end of the piece for the beginning of the armhole shaping.

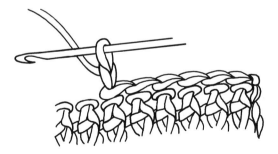

PRACTICE STITCHES WITH YARN

Now that you have practiced some of the various stitches and have learned to increase, decrease, and maintain the number of stitches on each row, it is time for you to try little swatches worked with yarn and larger hooks.

You will find that yarns split more easily than the heavy crochet thread you have been using. You will, however, get accustomed to working with yarns as you practice more with them. If the yarn splits, take the stitch out and carefully work the stitch again, making sure that you are not splitting the yarn again. Work back and forth until your piece of work looks even on the edges. Be sure to raise your work up to the level of the next row by chaining the number of stitches required for each of the kinds of stitches as follows:

1. When working single crochet stitches, you must chain one and turn.

2. When working half double crochet stitches, you must chain two and turn.

3. When working double crochet stitches, you must chain three and turn.

4. When working treble crochet stitches, you must chain four and turn.

5. When working double treble crochet stitches, you must chain five and turn.

6. When working triple treble crochet stitches, you must chain six and turn.

By now you must have observed that each of the stitches you have learned becomes progressively longer. The single crochet stitch is quite short, the half double crochet stitch, slightly longer, the double crochet stitch is longer than the half double, and so forth. By this method your pattern maker creates beautiful stitches for you. Sometimes you will be putting chain stitches in between some of the other stitches. Sometimes the pattern maker will prescribe several stitches to be placed in the same hole. All of this manipulating of the various simple stitches creates open and lacy stitches. Without the chains and the skips between stitches, you will form many of the sturdy patterns.

Joining New Thread

There will come a time when you will need to join a new ball of thread, or perhaps you will come upon a knot as the thread unwinds from the ball. You will not want any knots in your work. When it is time to join another thread, work whatever stitch is required in your pattern to the very last step of that stitch, using the last of the old thread. Then, take up the new thread and finish the last step of the stitch. The new thread has been joined without a knot. Place the two ends of thread to the wrong side of your piece of work. Later, when your pieces are completed, you will be instructed as to how to work in these ends. Be on the alert for weak places in threads or yarns and occasional flaws or knots. They should not be worked into your garment. Cut out the flaws or knots and start with a perfect piece of thread, working in as just described.

Note: If you are a knitter, you probably have made a practice of joining new yarn at the edges of your pieces in order to give a more perfect look to the inside of your garment. Later you made seams, and the joinings on the very edges were incased in the seams. Crochet pieces are more perfect on the edges. Many times a garment in crochet looks prettier if put together on the very edge; therefore, it is not a good idea to have any ends worked in on the edges. Ends in crochet can be easily hidden since crochet stitches are much more dense than knit stitches. For these reasons, it is advisable to work in ends on crochet through the body of the pieces. Keep all ends to the wrong side.

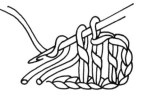

2 Starting the First Project

Conquering Fitting Problems

Choosing the Correct Size

Stitch Gauge: Why and How
   Directions for working an actual stitch gauge
   If you are off gauge . . .

Starting Your First Project
   Supply kit
   Abbreviations used in most pattern books
   Learning to read pattern books
   Diagram
     Key to diagram
     Sample diagram
     Use of yarn marker
     How to keep your place on the diagram

You Are Now Ready to Start Your First Project
   Working the second piece

2 Starting the First Project

CONQUERING FITTING PROBLEMS

You must learn to fit well, even on your first project. If you have had an unfortunate experience in crocheting—the garment did not fit properly when finished—the cause was one of two things or both. Either you did not choose the correct size from which to work, or you did not make an accurate stitch gauge. You can know to the inch what size your finished garment will be if you know how to choose the correct size and if you work an accurate stitch gauge. Since you do not have a paper pattern to lay upon your material, and you are making your own material, you must learn to figure mathematically what size you will need. Then you must learn to make an accurate stitch gauge. You must have your measurements taken, and from your measurements you can choose the size that is right for you in each different pattern. You must learn how to work an accurate stitch gauge and work one for *every* garment you make. All garments will need careful planning and preparation before you start. This may take a little more time, but a garment well planned and carefully checked as you proceed will block to the exact measurements. Then it will go together easily and can be finished beautifully. When you are finished, it will fit to your satisfaction. That will be your reward! Most people do not bother to do this extra bit of work, but if you do, you will be assured of a perfect-fitting garment. The mathematics involved is simple: addition, subtraction, multiplication, and division. You can learn to do this.

CHOOSING THE CORRECT SIZE

Do not guess at sizes and do not trust the measurement charts given either in the front or back of the pattern books. Sizes in crochet are not standardized. Pattern makers have their own idea as to size and they do not necessarily keep to the measurement charts. Crochet garments are not necessarily the size of ready-made clothes; therefore, you must not assume that size 12 will fit you if you wear size 12 in ready-made clothes. If, for example, you have already made a garment and the fit was good using a size 12 pattern, do not assume that all size 12s will fit you. If you have made a successful garment from a pattern book using a certain size, do not assume that all garments in *that* pattern book in that same size will fit the same as the first one. The book may have been made up of garments offered by many pattern makers, each person having different ideas as to size.

For a correct fit, you will need to know your actual measurement at the bustline. From your bust measurement, you will find the correct size for you for each garment you make. You must learn to figure the size mathematically. This is very simple to do. A certain amount of allowance over and above your actual bust measurement must be made. The allowance varies with the type of garment you intend to make and how heavy your yarn may be.

> *Example*: Actual bust measurement—34 inches.
> For a shell or a blouse, add approximately two inches—36 inches.
> For a Chanel jacket, use the actual measurement or add one inch—34 or 35 inches.
> For a buttoned jacket, add approximately three inches— 37 inches.

Note: The measurements must be taken in your slip if you are making a shell or a blouse. If you are making a jacket, measurements must be taken over the heaviest blouse or dress you are likely to wear under the jacket.

In order to choose the correct size, select from your pattern the size that you think will fit you. Then add up the stitches required for the front and back just before the underarm shaping. (Glance through the pattern until you find the number of stitches used just before the underarm shaping of the back. Jot down that number. Then glance through the directions given for the front or fronts, and find the number of stitches the pattern is using just before the underarm shaping.) Add the figures together and you will have the total number of stitches the pattern is using at the bustline. The next step is to divide the total number of stitches by the stitch gauge. This division will give you the size in inches of the finished garment. If the first size is too small for your measurements, plus the allowance, try the mathematics for the next size larger. If the first size is too large, try the mathematics for the next size smaller.

Note: If you are figuring for a buttoned jacket, you will need to read through the directions to find out how much border is added later. This information is usually found near the end of the pattern where finishing details are given. If, in the above example, for a buttoned jacket you need thirty-seven inches and you are adding one-inch borders, the total number of inches, through the body of the garment just before the underarm shaping, should be thirty-six inches. (Since one front border overlaps the other front border, you should count the inch of border stitches only once.)

Using the measurements in the example given on page 33 of "Actual bust measurement—34 inches,"

Your stitches added for a shell or blouse are
90 stitches—back
90 stitches—front
180 total

Now divide the total number of stitches (180) by the stitch gauge (given in your pattern) to get the finished measurement in inches. One hundred eighty stitches divided by five stitches per inch on the gauge equals thirty-six inches (the size).

$$\frac{180 \text{ stitches}}{5 \text{ stitches per inch}} \quad \text{equals 36 inches, or size 36}$$

Your stitches added for a Chanel jacket are
85 stitches—back
45 stitches—front
45 stitches—front
175 total

Now divide the total number of stitches (175) by the stitch gauge (given in your pattern) to get the finished measurement in inches. One hundred seventy-five stitches divided by five stitches per inch on the gauge equals thirty-five inches (the size).

$$\frac{175 \text{ stitches}}{5 \text{ stitches per inch}} \quad \text{equals 35 inches, or size 35}$$

Your stitches added for a buttoned jacket are
88 stitches—back
46 stitches—front
46 stitches—front
180 total

Now divide the total number of stitches (180) by the stitch gauge (given in your pattern) to get the finished measurement in inches. One hundred eighty stitches divided by five stitches per inch on the gauge equals thirty-six inches. (When the one-inch border has been added, the size will be 37.)

$$\frac{180 \text{ stitches}}{5 \text{ stitches per inch}} \quad \text{equals 36 inches, or size 36}$$

Note: In reading through the directions for the number of stitches required on the back and fronts, keep in mind that some patterns may require increases up the sides *before* the underarm shaping; therefore, make sure that you add the correct number of stitches *just before* the shaping of the underarm. If the first size you tried out was not correct, keep trying the various sizes until you come upon a size closest to the size that you need.

STITCH GAUGE: WHY AND HOW

A stitch gauge is a sample of your crocheting which enables you to find out how many stitches per inch you are getting. Because all patterns are based on a given number of stitches per inch, you must work a sample gauge for every garment you make before you start the garment. You must match your gauge to the gauge given in the pattern; or your finished project will not be the size you chose to make. You can know exactly what size your finished garment will be if you obtain the gauge given in the pattern. You must never assume that you are an average crocheter and therefore do not need to work a gauge. You may crochet tighter or looser than the pattern maker, and if so, your hook size will need to be changed so that you obtain the same gauge as the pattern maker. When working your gauge, be sure to use the yarn you intend to use for your finished garment. Sometimes yarns will vary in weight, even in the same brand of yarn. Occasionally the dyeing process may make the yarn heavier or lighter. Do not be careless about working gauges. Use the tension you regularly use. Do not try to tighten or loosen the stitches to make the work come out to the needed gauge. It is better to adjust your hook size (either larger or smaller, as the case may be) than to try to work with a tension other than your regular tension. Before long, you would return to your regular tension, and then your whole piece would be off gauge. Learn to work an accurate gauge.

Directions for Working an Accurate Stitch Gauge

A gauge must be worked for *every* garment. A four-inch gauge is the only accurate gauge. Take the hook size suggested in the pattern and make the foundation chain equal to the number of stitches required for a four-inch piece.

Example: A gauge of four double crochet stitches equals one inch.

You will chain eighteen stitches for your foundation row—the two extra stitches are required because you will work one double crochet stitch in the fourth chain from the hook and one double crochet stitch in each chain across the row, counting until you have made sixteen double crochet stitches in all. Refresh your memory on the double crochet stitch by reviewing page 16. Work across the first row, working sixteen double crochet stitches. Chain three to count as the first double crochet stitch for the next row. Work row after row of double crochet stitches.

Caution! Be sure to make your foundation chain quite loose. Since you are carefully working a gauge, you will not want your foundation row to draw in your swatch at the bottom edge.

As another example, if your pattern reads, "three patterns equals one inch," you will need to follow the directions in your pattern book to find out how to make the stitches. Then work a large enough sample of the pattern stitch to equal at least four inches. If the pattern stitch consists of several different rows, work enough rows to complete the pattern sequence several times. It is advisable to measure your gauge before and after blocking. Therefore, measure your gauge, counting out enough stitches to equal four inches—sixteen stitches would be required for the above example of four double crochet stitches equals one inch. Make a notation of the measurement on a piece of paper.

Next, you should block your gauge by getting it completely wet in cold water. Block your gauge quite wet. Lay the gauge on a piece of toweling. Stretch the gauge out width-wise and make the edges straight and even. Next, work with the length, bringing the

Stitch Gauge

piece down so that it is not stretched more in one direction than the other. Press the gauge with the palm of your hand. Set the piece aside to dry. When the gauge is completely dry, measure out four inches and count the number of stitches in the four inches. If you were to obtain a gauge of four double crochet stitches equals one inch, sixteen double crochet stitches should equal four inches. If you are to meet a gauge in the other example of "three patterns equals one inch," count out twelve patterns. The twelve patterns should measure four inches. If you do not meet the gauge and the piece measures less than four inches, try the next size larger hook and work another gauge. If the piece measures more than four inches, try another gauge with the next size smaller hook. Write down the before and after blocking measurements. State what hook size was used. Pin this to the sample gauge. You should be concerned with how the gauge measures in width more than how the gauge measures in length. Usually, if you meet the gauge width-wise you will also meet the gauge lengthwise. If you do not meet the gauge lengthwise, you will need to work more or fewer rows. *You must meet the gauge width-wise, or the garment will not fit your figure.*

There may be considerable stretch in your work, and you can find out approximately how much stretch there is when you block your gauge. Since you will be washing and blocking your garment, and not sending it to a dry-cleaner, you will be concerned with how the garment will fit *after* the washing and blocking processes; therefore, your stitch gauge must be wet and blocked, and then dried before you decide upon the gauge. Many yarns may stretch and "grow" when wet. In many cases, a gauge measuring four inches before blocking will measure four and one-fourth inches after blocking. You must know this so that your hook size can be adjusted. It is most important that your gauge measure four inches *after* it has been wet and dried. It is advisable to measure your gauge before and after blocking. Make a notation of the measurements before and after, and pin that information to your gauge. This information will be useful as a comparison when proceeding with your work.

If You Are off Gauge

The reason a four-inch gauge is recommended is because it gives you a large enough sample of your work so that you will not deceive yourself into thinking you are on gauge. If you should work a one- or a two-inch gauge, you can push the work together or spread the work apart and make the gauge come out to the one- or two-inch measurement. But with a four-inch gauge, if you are off one-fourth inch in four inches, that will be only a fraction of a stitch per inch. These fractions of stitches add up to stitches, and stitches add up to inches. If you were off one-fourth inch in a four-inch piece, you would be off one-half inch in an eight-inch piece, and one whole inch in sixteen inches. If you were striving for a size 36, you would gain two and one-fourth inches. Your garment would measure thirty-eight and one-fourth inches. If your gauge was off in the other direction, you would be loosing one-fourth inch in four inches, one-half inch in eight inches, one inch in sixteen inches, and so forth. The entire garment would be two and one-fourth inches too small, measuring thirty-three and three-fourths inches. You should remember that it is the fraction of a stitch which may make the difference.

STARTING YOUR FIRST PROJECT

Now you have learned to crochet many of the basic crochet stitches, and you have practiced long enough so that you have the proper tension on your yarn and your stitches look quite even. You know how to increase, decrease, and bind off. You know how to maintain the number of stitches required. You are now ready to start your first project. Practice on yourself first. Select a pattern for a simple shell (a sleeveless blouse) for your first project. Simple lines require less shaping. Do not be tempted by a pattern requiring difficult crochet stitches that you are not familiar with. A wool yarn is the best material to use for this first project, since it is easier to control in the blocking process. Choose a light or a bright color so that you can see the stitches form and be able to count your stitches easily. Buy a pattern from a reliable pattern company. Use the best quality yarns. Yarns of poor quality may streak, run, fade, shrink, or stretch. Pattern books and yarns put out by a good yarn company are reliable and show the latest fashions.

Supply Kit

Purchase a bag to keep all of your materials together and ready to use. The supplies you will need are:

Tape measure (use plastic or fiber glass)
Crochet hooks of various sizes
Straight pins
Safety pins
Scraps of different-colored yarns or threads
    (for yarn markers)
Pair of scissors
Tapestry needles
Sewing needles and basting threads
Scratch pad and pencil

Caution! Make sure that the yarn you intend to use for yarn markers is of good quality. These markers remain in the garment through the washing and blocking processes, and poor quality yarns may fade or run on your crochet pieces.

Abbreviations Used in Most Pattern Books

st	stitch
sts	stitches
ch	chain
sc	single crochet
hdc	half double crochet
dc	double crochet
tr	treble crochet
dtr	double treble crochet
tr tr	triple treble crochet
sp	space
sk	skip

sl st	slip stitch
cl	cluster
P	picot
lp	loop
rnd	round
inc	increase
dec	decrease
pat	pattern
tog	together
yo	yarn over or thread over
beg	beginning
✢	repeat instructions, following the asterisk as many times as specified

Learning to Read Pattern Books

You must learn to read every comma, period, and semicolon, etc. when reading directions in pattern books. Many people have difficulty in doing this because they do not understand that the work must be done in many small steps. Each step is set off by commas, semicolons, and periods. When the pattern maker directs you to do a certain step and place a stitch in a certain place, she is referring to the row *below* where you are to place the stitch—not through a stitch on the row on which you are working. As an example, you will occasionally be directed to work "1 dc in second sc, ch 4, 1 dc in top of dc just made." In a case such as this, you will place a double crochet stitch in the second single crochet stitch of the previous row, chain four, then place a double crochet stitch on top of the double crochet stitch that you just finished making on the same row. Use the pin method for reading and working patterns, as explained on page 72. The pin holds your place and your hands are free to work step by step through the pattern.

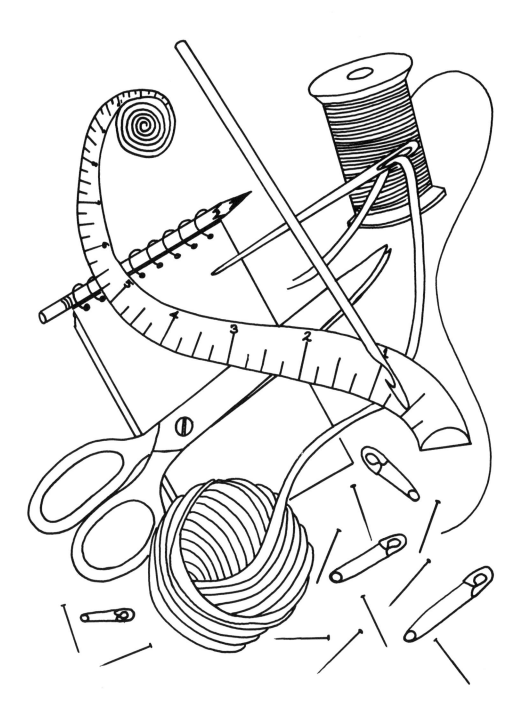

Undoubtedly the pattern you have selected to use as your first project may be used for several sizes. Your pattern will state the various sizes which can be made from the pattern. Most pattern books give fairly complete directions, and a key to reading these directions is given at the start of the pattern. Usually the smallest size instructions are given first, then parentheses are used for the other sizes.

Example: "Directions are for size 10. Changes for sizes 12, 14, and 16 are in parentheses." As you are reading through the pattern, notice that you may be asked to start out with a chain of 81 (85-89-93) stitches. If you are making the size 10, you will use the first number—81 stitches. If you are making the size 12, you will use 85 stitches; for size 14, 89 stitches, and for size 16, 93 stitches. All through the pattern you will be given numbers such as the 81 (85-89-93), and you must use the number referring to the size from which you have chosen to work. If the pattern calls for several different weights of yarns, determine which group your yarn is in. Make sure you are reading the correct column. Make sure you are picking up the numbers for *your* size. An excellent method is to circle your size throughout the pattern.

If you have not read through the directions for choosing the correct size and for working an accurate stitch gauge, be sure to do so now. Make sure that you understand why you must do both of these things for every garment you make. You must understand that you are making your own material. But you have no paper pattern to lay on your material, and you cannot cut your material if you have made it too large. You must crochet each piece properly to your own measurements. Do not guess at lengths. Use your own lengths. All of this information must appear on your pattern page.

Take out your pattern book and put down your actual size (your actual bust measurement) in the upper left-hand corner of the book on the page where your directions are found. Then, on the right-hand corner of the same page, put down your crochet measurements.

Actual size 36	Crochet size	−39
	Length	−14
	Sleeve length	−15
	Overall	−
	Overall sleeve	−

Of course, you will be putting your own measurements onto this chart. These measurements will be in front of you while you are working your garment. You may want to check the measurements from time to time as you are progressing.

Before you start your project, learn the abbreviations used in pattern books. Do exactly what is said. Remember, you are shaping the pieces of your garment, and when the pattern asks that you bind off or decrease, this means that you are shaping for armholes, shoulders, the neck, and so forth.. You will start to *see* pieces being formed.

Diagram

Learn to draw a diagram and use one for everything you crochet. A simple diagram will show you the shape of the pieces, and it will tell you where and when to shape. Using a diagram will improve your work 100 percent and you will make fewer mistakes. You will work and measure more accurately. When you learn to keep your place on the diagram, you can set your work aside for several days and still tell at a glance where you left off. Learn to draw a large diagram so that your markings will not be crowded. If you are to be helped by this diagram, you must be able to read it easily.

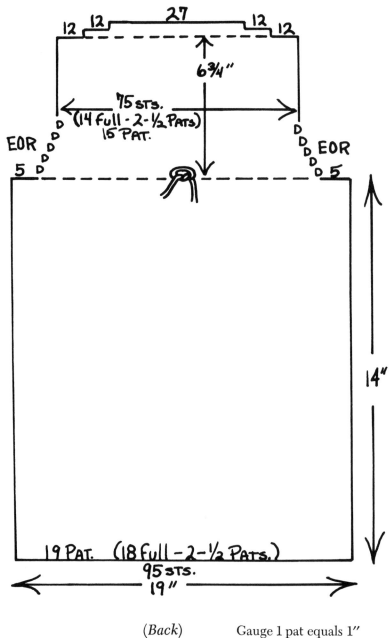

12   12   27   12   12

6¾"

75 STS.
(14 Full - 2-½ Pats)
15 Pat.

EOR   EOR

5   5

19 Pat.   (18 Full - 2-½ Pats.)
95 STS.
19"

14"

(*Back*)   Gauge 1 pat equals 1"
                      5 dc equals 1"

KEY TO DIAGRAM

D	Decrease
I	Increase
ER	Every row
EOR	Every other row
PAT	Pattern, patterns
4	Bind off or slip stitch
	Yarn marker

SAMPLE DIAGRAM

The following instructions will be used for the sample diagram: Chain 96 loosely to measure 19 inches. Sc in 2nd ch from hook and in each ch across—95 sts. Ch 1, turn. Work in pattern with 19 pat (18 full pats and two half pats), across to 14 inches from beg, or desired length to underarm, ending on pat row 4.

Shape armholes: Sl st across 5 sts, work in pat until 5 sts from other end. 17 pat. (16 full pats and 2 half pats.) Dec 1 st each side every other row 5 times. 75 sts. 15 pat. (14 full pats and 2 half pats.) Work even until armhole measures 6¾″.

Shape shoulders: Sl st across 12 sts, work in pat to within 12 sts of end of row, ch 1, turn. Sl st across 12 sts, work to within 12 sts of end of row. Fasten off. (See drawing.)

USE OF YARN MARKER

You must be very precise when measuring armholes. Never measure around the curve of the armhole. Measure straight up from the row of the first bound-off stitches. Tie in a marker on the row of the first bind-off near the center of your work. Place the marker

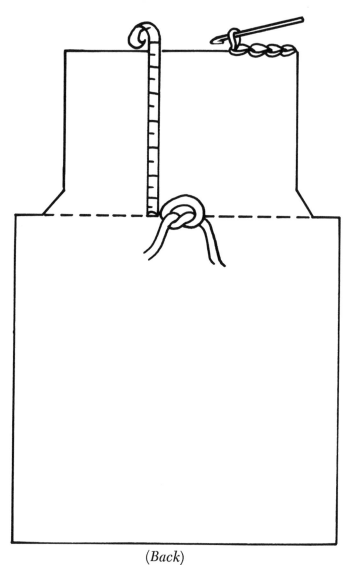

(Back)

on the right side (outside) of the piece. (See drawing.) If your garment is to have sleeves, the sleeves will not fit into the arm-hole properly *unless* the armhole is measured exactly as the pattern states.

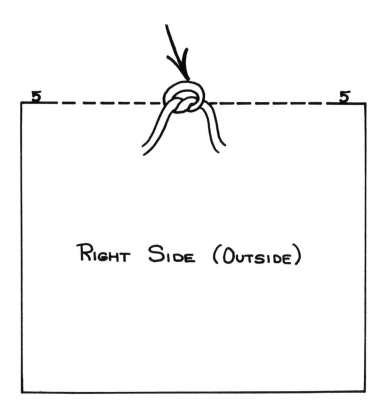

HOW TO KEEP YOUR PLACE ON THE DIAGRAM

You will know where you are at all times if you get into the habit of circling each part of the diagram as you work it.

Example: As you slip stitch across five stitches at the beginning of the armhole shaping, circle the 5. Tie in your marker near the center of the piece. After you have worked across the row to within the five stitches of the other end of the piece, also circle the 5 at this end of your piece. Work across the next wrong side row; then start the decreases, circling the Ds as you do them. If

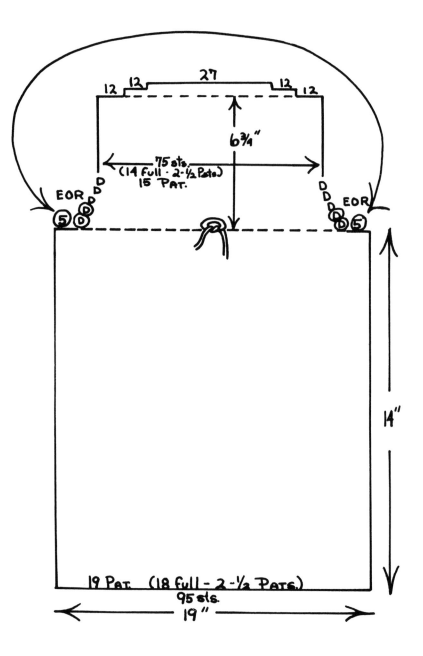

12 12 27 12 12

6¾″

75 sts.
(14 full · 2 ½ Pats.)
15 Pat.

EOR D D D   D D D EOR
5 D   D 5

14″

19 Pat. (18 full − 2 · ½ Pats.)
95 sts.
19″

you should have to lay your work aside after any shaping, you can quickly tell where to start in again. The work which has been circled is finished; the work not circled is yet to be done.

Note: Review bind-off on page 27. When working the decreases, use the regulation decrease method, which is explained on page 23. (If the pattern maker wishes you to use some other method of decreasing, step-by-step instructions will be given in your pattern.)

YOU ARE NOW READY TO START YOUR FIRST PROJECT

After choosing your correct size, working and blocking your accurate stitch gauge, and drawing your diagram, you should start the back of your shell. When you have finished the first row, mark it on the right side with a scrap of colored yarn. Lengths in crochet garments present a serious problem. Crochet pieces often stretch in length (more than the four-inch gauge stretched in length). It seems that gravity works on the pieces, and the longer the pieces become, the more stretch in length you may have. It is advisable, therefore, to stop a little short of the underarm shaping and block the piece. Wet the piece completely in cold water; then lay the piece out on a Turkish towel, with the right side up and the wrong side down. Block the piece to the desired width at the underarm and at the bottom edge. Consult your pattern page where you have put down your personal crochet measurements. After you have obtained the desired width, bring the piece down and up with the palms of your hands as far as you can stretch the piece and still maintain the width measurement. In this way, you will be getting all of the stretch out of your piece. Let the piece dry completely. Take the length measurement again, and if your garment "grew" in length, you may have to take out a few rows before shaping the underarms. It is better to know if the garment is going to stretch in length *now*, when it will be easy to make the correction, than to finish the back and find that it is several inches too long. Then you must rip back to the underarm shaping, remove the excess rows, and then finish the piece again. Less ripping is involved if you block from time to time.

Resume your work again, ripping rows or working more rows—whichever is necessary. Now you have a very good idea as to how the entire garment will block.

Now that you have made a long sample of your work, which has been blocked, it is time for you to measure your armhole depth. Measure on the blocked part of your garment. For example, if you work to six and three-fourths inches above the armhole shaping, measure out six and three-fourths inches on the blocked portion of your garment. Count that number of rows or patterns, and work *that* number of rows or patterns above the armhole. All measurements from now on should be taken on the blocked portion; rows or patterns should be counted, using *this* number of rows or patterns, rather than measuring directly on the unblocked portion where you are working.

Working the Second Piece

After the back is finished and you are working the front, be sure to work the front piece the same length as the back. Count the rows or patterns to insure that you have equal rows. When you stitch the pieces together, you will be joining each row by matching.

You must be very careful that you are working with the same tension on the second piece so that the pieces will be the same width and length. Measure and compare the second piece to the first piece. You may want to block part way along on the second piece, as you did on the first piece. If you find that the second piece is narrower than the first piece, using the same number of stitches, you will have to start again, disciplining yourself to maintain the same gauge.

To be on the safe side, even though you worked an accurate stitch gauge, you should check your stitch gauge periodically to be sure you are maintaining the same tension. You will have portions of blocked and unblocked work to use as a comparison as you proceed. After working several rows, stop and take the first check on the gauge. Many people work tighter or looser as they become more familiar with the stitch and are working faster. You may have to slow down to make the stitches conform to the work of the first piece. Your first concern is to obtain evenness—not speed. *You must maintain your stitch gauge.*

Most patterns will require that you work the front piece the same as the back piece until it is time to shape the front neck. It is best to draw a diagram for the entire front. In this way, you will be able to circle all of the underarm shaping as you work along. The instructions that were used as an example for the back diagram continue on for the front:

> Front—work same as back until armhole measures 4 inches, ending on pat row 4. Shape neck: Work across 29 sts, ch 3 turn. Work in pattern st, decreasing 1 st at neck edge every other row 5 times, shaping shoulders same as back when armhole is same length. Fasten off. Skip 17 sts for front of neck, attach yarn in next st, ch 3, work in pattern to end of row (29 sts). Complete to correspond to first side.

Draw your diagram for the front. See drawing on page 55. Work the underarm shaping as you did on the back, circling all of your markings as you did before. Now, when your armhole measures four inches from the armhole marker, it is time to shape the neck. Work across the twenty-nine stitches from the right side of your work. You will need to work each piece separately now until the left neck and shoulder has been completed. You will then count across seventeen stitches for the center front neck and attach your yarn in the next stitch to work the other half of the front (the right half). Be sure to count rows above the yarn marker (placed on the row of the first bind-off for the underarm), and work as many rows before shaping the shoulders as you worked on the back. Now you will be working and finishing one half of the front before you start the other half. To simplify this procedure, label the left section of the front B, and the right section of the front A. Hold the piece of crochet to your body with the right side out to make sure you have labeled them correctly. Take little scraps of paper and pin them directly on your crochet pieces on each side, right and left. (After you have done this once or twice on future garments, you probably will not need to label the separate sides.)

Note: You will need to add new yarn markers, since your yarn marker was originally placed in the center and your center stitches have been bound off. Place a marker in the center of each side, as they are placed on the diagram, so that you can measure or count rows from the markers on the separate sides.

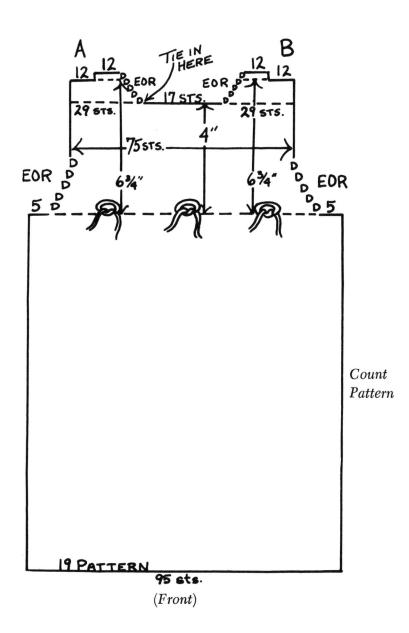

A

B

12   12

TIE IN HERE

12   12

EOR

EOR

17 STS.

29 STS.

29 STS.

75 STS.

4"

EOR

EOR

5

6¾"

6¾"

5

Count
Pattern

19 PATTERN

95 sts.

(*Front*)

3 Finishing the First Project

Preparation before Assembling
    Working in ends
    Washing
        Washing do's and don'ts
    Blocking

Assembling
    Proper sequence
    Fine points of assembling
        Method of steaming seams
        Sewing the side seams
        Setting in sleeves

3 Finishing the First Project

PREPARATION BEFORE ASSEMBLING

After the pieces of your garment are finished, they should be carefully checked to make sure that they match and that they are shaped correctly. Lay like pieces together and make sure that they are the same width and length. When you are sure that the pieces have been worked correctly, you are ready to wash, block, and assemble them. All trims—collars, pockets, and edgings, etc. —are worked after blocking.

After matching the pieces, you must make a note of the overall back measurement (and the overall sleeve measurement, if your garment has sleeves). In order to get the accurate overall measurement, you must add the length of the garment from the marker to the hem and the measurement of the upper half of your garment. In the example used on page 46, the garment was to be worked for six and three-fourths inches above the armhole marker before shaping the shoulders. Now, count the number of rows (or patterns) you worked from the marker to the finish of the shoulders on your completed back piece. Since there was a nice long portion of blocked work to measure on, count out the same number of rows (or patterns) on the blocked portion and measure with your tape measure to get the amount, in inches, that the upper portion should measure. Add the two measurements together (lower and upper portions). This is your overall measurement. Write the overall measurements on the chart you were to have made, as shown in the example on page 45. When you are blocking your completed pieces, you will need to know these overall measurements as well as your other measurements so that you can block the armholes to the right lengths.

The yarn markers you used for right-side markers, or the markers used for armhole lengths, must *not* be removed before washing and blocking. However, do remove any safety pins, if you used any to designate right sides, and replace them with yarn markers. The reason for this is that safety pins may leave a smudge or a discoloration on your crochet pieces if the pieces are wet.

Working in Ends

All ends must be worked in before washing and blocking. If you added new yarn according to the instructions given on page 29, you will not have any knots to untie. If you tied in knots, you will

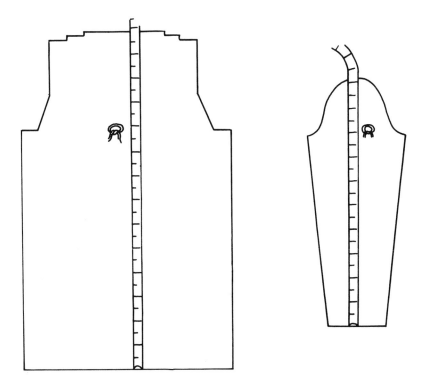

need to untie them now. You will not want any knots left in your garment to disgrace you. Bring all loose threads to the wrong side, thread a tapestry needle with one of the ends, and weave the needle through the posts of double crochet stitches, or any of the longer stitches. Weave the needle farther than just through the post. Weave the needle along the tops of stitches in the row below for approximately one inch. Then turn back and weave over the same area for about one-half inch. Snip off any remaining thread close to the stitches. Work in the other end in the same manner, but in the opposite direction, so that you will not have the two ends worked in in the same place. (See drawing.)

If you have ends from chain stitches that need to be worked in, thread a tapestry needle with one thread and weave the needle through the chains until you come to some firmer work, then proceed as just directed. Work in the second end in the opposite direction. Try to eliminate the working in of ends on the very edges of your garment. If there are any ends on the side edges where you will later form seams, move the ends in several stitches from the edge on the wrong side of your work, and then work in the ends as just described. Since you will be seaming your pieces together on the very edges, you will not want any ends worked in on these edges. You will be surprised at how well the ends will be concealed, because all of your stitches are quite dense and the ends are easily hidden. After the pieces have been blocked, the ends seem to disappear into the work.

Washing

Do not attempt to assemble crochet pieces that have not been washed and blocked. It is easy to block to the exact measurements while your garment is in pieces, and it is very difficult to block to these measurements if the garment has been seamed together. The seams tend to hold the garment to the size it was before seaming. To give a professional look to your work, you should always block the pieces first and then add the trim during assembling.

Since you will need to completely wet your crochet pieces in order to block them, why not wash them first? All crochet pieces get soiled while you are working on them. If you wash the pieces, your garment, when completed, will look brand new and clean. Water and sweater soap are good for woolens. On the other hand, solvents or cleaning fluids tend to take the natural elasticity from some fibers and the colors may become grayish after many cleanings. Water will not harm yarns if they are washed properly. Most hand-knitting and crocheting yarns are washable. If your yarn is not washable, the label will state that it must be dry-cleaned only.

After many hours of painstaking work crocheting your garment pieces, it would be most regrettable if you should ruin them in the washing process. Learn to use the proper washing method. Study the Do's and Don'ts which follow. All of the Don'ts produce serious side effects, such as streaking, fading, running, or shrinking.

WASHING DO'S AND DON'TS

Do's	*Don'ts*
Use cold water.	Never use warm water.
Use a good sweater soap.	Never use excessive amounts of soap.
Use the amount of soap the manufacturer recommends.	Never oversoak.
Allow the pieces to soak three minutes.	Never rub the pieces together.
Handle the pieces very gently.	Do not hold the pieces up and let them sag.
Swish the pieces around in the suds.	Never leave pieces rolled up in a towel.

Press out the soapy water (bring the pieces to the edge of the bowl and gently push out the soapy water).

Rinse at least four times in cold water.

Press out excess moisture.

Lay the pieces out on a turkish towel.

Block immediately.

To hasten drying, change the towels under the pieces twice a day.

Never dry in the sun or near direct heat.

Blocking

Pieces will block nicely if you leave lots of moisture in them. Do not roll the pieces in a towel until you are ready to block each piece. You may want to set the wet pieces in a large bowl or dishpan until you are ready to block them. Then each piece should be rolled in a towel very quickly to leave it quite wet. If you remove most of the moisture from the pieces before blocking, they will be stubborn and will refuse to conform to your measurements. There will be many wrinkles in the piece and you cannot remove them. Re-wet the piece so that you can control it.

Block the pieces in a place where they will not be disturbed during the drying process. Use clean padding under the pieces to absorb moisture; towels or pieces of quilted bed pads will do nicely. Lay out your crochet measurements (those you jotted down at the top of the pattern page). Start with the back piece and lay it out with the right side up. Smooth it from the center out until it meets the measurements you have jotted down. The back should measure half of the crochet measurement at the bust. (For crochet measurement thirty-eight, block the back out to nineteen inches.) Next, bring the piece down until the length is correct. Always measure from the yarn marker to the exact length of your crochet measurements. If the piece is too short, work from the center, pushing up and down. Use the palms of your hands in a smoothing motion. Check the overall measurement next. If the overall measurement is not the exact length you jotted down, the adjustment must be made in the upper portion (opposite the armhole), measuring up from the yarn marker. When you are sure the measurements conform, work with all of the edges, pinching them to a straight line. Rub out any unevenness with your fingers and then "press" the piece all over with the palms of your hands to make it flat.

Note: If you are having trouble making the crochet pieces wide enough (that is, as soon as you take your hands off the

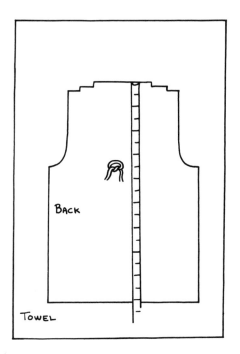

pieces, they begin to creep back in again), weight down the edges with something heavy, such as drinking glasses, fruit jars, or pop bottles. Do not pin the pieces down. It is too hard to remove the little peak marks left by the pins after the pieces are dry, and this makes it difficult to seam the pieces together.

You are now ready to work with the front piece (which was worked the same as the back except for the front neck shaping). Carefully lay the front on top of the back with the right side facing you and with the wrong side down on the back. You will not need to measure the front because you carefully measured the back piece. Like pieces are blocked together so that they will be exactly alike. Make sure that the edges are straight and even and that the lengths are the same. If you are making a jacket with two front pieces, lay each front on top of the back as is shown in the illustration. If there are sleeves, block them now. First do one sleeve, laying it out as you did the back, to the measurements. The width of a lady's sleeve before the start of the cap shaping should be at least fourteen inches (or divide the number of

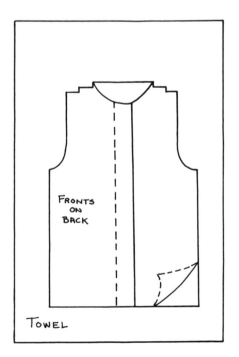

FRONTS
ON
BACK

TOWEL

stitches [or patterns] on the piece at that point by your stitch gauge to get the exact measurement). Measure lengths accurately from the yarn markers. Make sure that the overall measurement is correct. Then lay the other sleeve out on top of the first sleeve. Since the sleeves are shaped the same for right or left, you may either lay the sleeves out right sides together or with the right sides up.

You will want to change the towels under your blocked pieces after about a half day. Gravity seems to pull the water out of the pieces and into the towels. Carefully move the pieces over and exchange the wet towels for dry ones. After you lay the pieces out on the dry towels, check on the measurements again. Sometimes, as the pieces are drying, they may draw in somewhat. If this happens, weight down the edges as suggested on page 64.

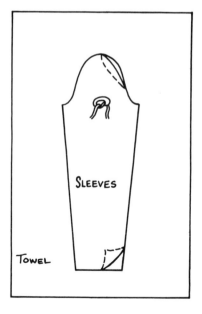

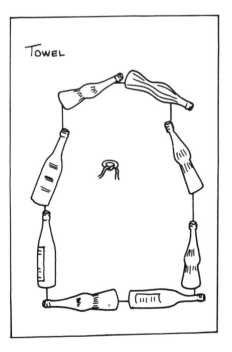

ASSEMBLING

Now that you have crocheted your garment pieces and have washed and blocked them, you will want to assemble them meticulously so that the finished project will not have a homemade look. This work takes time and it is tedious and monotonous. Work done in a hurry can easily ruin an otherwise beautiful garment. You can achieve a professional look with practice and correct methods.

Crochet garments may be put together in many different ways. If you are a knitter, you probably have put your knit garments together with a seam, using the backstitch approximately one-fourth inch in from the edge, or picking up the *eye*. This method would not be good to use to join crochet work because most crochet work is quite open and lacy. You would constantly come upon holes in the work where you could not stitch. For this reason, most seams in crochet are made by butting the edges together. If two bound-off edges are to be joined, then you will form a very small flat seam, placing your stitches in the center of each of the bound-off stitches. Try some of the methods which will be explained in detail. Practice them on your crochet swatches. In this way, you will have a little experience before commencing on your garment.

Proper Sequence

For best results, the proper construction sequence should be used. If the garment is sleeveless or has set-in sleeves, sew the shoulder seams first. Then set in the sleeve as a flat piece. Sew the sleeve and body seam next. Finally, add the crochet trim, collar, pockets, and so forth.

If the garment is a jacket with raglan sleeves, sew all of the raglan seams first. Then sew the sleeve and body seam all in one.

The yarn to use for sewing should be of a lighter weight than the yarn used for crocheting the garment. However, you will want an exact match in color and texture so that the stitches will disappear into the work. You can split four-ply yarn into two-ply and use two-ply for seaming. If the yarn is three-ply, take one strand away and discard it, and use two-ply for seaming. By making the sewing thread finer, you will be able to make prettier seams. Heavy, bulky seams are unattractive. Use a small tapestry needle for sewing the seams. Fine yarns and fine needles make fine seams. Do not use long strands of yarn for seaming because the yarn will become weak before it is all used. Use a piece no longer than eighteen inches. Do not use any knots to start or end the seams. Knots have a way of working through to the right side of the garment and they spoil the professional look you are trying to achieve. Use an over-and-over stitch near where you will start and end the seams. This will give you a strong beginning and ending without the use of knots. Each seam must be steamed carefully before any cross seams are made.

Fine Points of Assembling

Most of the seams will have to be made with the right side (outside) of the garment facing you. You will be doing a stitch similar to a lacing stitch. Start with the shoulder seam first. Anchor the thread on one shoulder close to the edge of one of the pieces, and then weave the needle through threads to get to the edge. Work from the armhole toward the neck. Pin the two pieces together so that the stitches match. Since you have the same number of stitches on each shoulder edge, you must match stitch for stitch.

Note: Examine the edges of the shoulders you wish to seam. You will see that there is a row of loops resembling a chain across the top of each of the two pieces you want to sew together. If you were to sew on the very edge, two chains would show after the

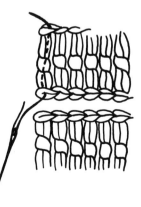

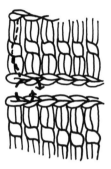

seam is completed. You will want only *one* chain to show; therefore, you must conceal half of each chain on the inside of the seam on each piece. Take a very small stitch through the center of the chain on one shoulder piece; then take a small stitch through the center of the chain on the other piece. (See drawing.) With the thumbnail, push both edges to the wrong side to form a *very small flat seam*. Continue to take stitch for stitch until you reach the other end of the seam. Fasten off the thread by using the over-and-over stitch (the same stitch you used to anchor the thread at the beginning). Now steam the seam.

METHOD OF STEAMING SEAMS

Do not iron crochet pieces. The weight of the iron must never rest on the piece. The ironing board should be heavily padded with Turkish toweling. You may use either a steam or a dry iron. You will be making your own steam with a wet Turkish washcloth. Make sure the setting of the iron is *no hotter than "wool."* An iron which is too hot may cause a color change on the part of the garment you are steaming. Place the seam to be steamed on the padded ironing board, with the wrong side of the garment facing you and the right side down on the board. Place a wet washcloth over the seam to be steamed. The washcloth must be quite wet, otherwise you will be unable to make the steam penetrate into the crochet material. Touch the wet washcloth with the iron and hold it in place for several seconds. You will hear a sizzling sound. Do *not* let the weight of the iron rest on the washcloth. Hold back the weight of the iron so that you do not press the crochet seam. You want to make steam only. After you have held the iron in position for a few seconds, remove the washcloth and gently press the seam with your fingers. The seam will look pressed, but your work will not look ironed or matted. *Never* iron directly any part of the crochet pieces. When steaming synthetics set iron accordingly and use extra caution.

If you must steam a sleeve seam or any curved seam, you will need to do the work in many small steps in order to get around the curves and not stretch the piece in any other place. Keep the seam close to the edge and the point of the ironing board so that you will not press any folds in other parts of the garment. You may wish to set a card table under your ironing board to support parts of the drooping pieces as you work near the edge and point of the ironing board.

Note: The washcloth must be quite wet at all times or you cannot make the steam you need. You will find that you are continually wetting the cloth. Therefore, it is advisable to have a bowl of water handy. Use a small piece of Turkish toweling (washcloth) rather than a large piece. A large piece would drip all over other parts of your garment.

SEWING THE SIDE SEAMS

Before you sew the side seams, notice that all stitches in crochet are joined at the top and at the bottom of the stitch. When you are working a row of half double crochet stitches, the stitch is joined at the top and bottom to the next stitch, but there is a small post in between that is not joined. When you are working a double crochet stitch, it too is joined to the adjacent stitch at the top and bottom of the stitch. The post, which is slightly longer than the half double crochet stitch, is not joined. When you seam two pieces of crochet work together, you will want to tack the two pieces together at the top and bottom of the stitches. The posts will not be joined (they are free through the middle of the posts). By joining in this way, your crochet pieces will have a more invisible joining and the work will look almost as if there is no seam. After placing a little "tack" stitch, you must run your needle and thread through the post or the chain of the next stitch so that it will not be seen. When you come to the top of the next stitch, join again with another tack stitch. Since you

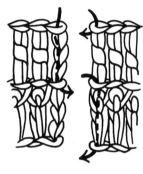

have the same number of rows on the front and back sections, you will tack at the top of each row. Slip your needle and thread through the post of the stitch below and tack again at the top of the next row. Continue in this manner, matching row after row until you come to the bottom edge. Make a firm tack stitch at the bottom. Run your needle and thread a short way up from the end of the seam and fasten off. Steam the seam.

Caution! Since there is stretch in the whole garment, you will want a little stretch on the seams. Therefore, as you are placing your tack stitches on the seam, make sure that you are not drawing in the seam to make it rigid. Stretch out the seam from time to time to make sure that the seam is not taut.

Note: If your garment has sleeves, set in the sleeves *before* the side seams are sewed. (See below.)

SETTING IN SLEEVES

After the shoulder seam has been seamed and steamed, you are ready to set in the sleeves. The sleeve should be set in as a flat piece. *Note*: It is much easier to ease in any fullness and to steam the armhole seam if the side seams of the garment have not been sewed first.

Find the middle of the cap of the sleeve by folding the sleeve in half. Pin the center to the shoulder seam. Place pins all around the armhole, easing in any fullness. Start at one end and make little tack stitches, as explained on page 69. You will not be able to match row for row, however, because your sleeve cap is rounded by decreases on the edge. Work from the right side of the garment, taking little tack stitches through the top of each stitch on the garment piece and a little tack stitch on the sleeve piece. Occasionally, you will have to take tack stitches through posts on the sleeve piece since the rows do not match. Steam the seam before sewing the sleeve and body seam.

For finishing details see page 169.

4 Pattern Stitches

Learning How to Read Pattern Stitches
    Asterisk
    Double asterisks
    Dagger
    Parentheses

Explanation of Different Pattern Stitches

Pattern Stitches
    V stitch
    Shell and V stitch
    Shell stitch
    Staggered shell stitch
    Slant shell stitch
    Picot stitch
    Popcorn stitch
    Cluster stitch
    Puff stitch
    Cross puff stitch
    Star stitch
    Knot stitch (Lover's knot stitch)
    Loop stitch
    Double loop stitch
    Roll stitch
    Around-the-post stitch
    Filet crochet
    Cross stitch
    Cross treble crochet stitch

Crocheting Colored Designs

4 Pattern Stitches

LEARNING HOW TO READ PATTERN STITCHES

Reading crochet patterns is not always easy. Pattern makers are very precise in their directions—and also very concise. They do not give step-by-step instructions on how to do the stitches; everything is kept brief and they assume that you know the basics of crocheting. One of the hardest problems is keeping your place in the pattern. You must work step-by-step through the pattern sequence several times before you will be able to work that row without using the printed directions.

Use the "straight pin method" for reading pattern stitches. (See drawing.) Read and do the work by many little steps. Read a few phrases; then stick a straight pin into the page to show you where your place is; then do that much work. Then read the next phrase, move the pin, and so forth. With this method, your hands are free to do the work and the pin holds your place in the book.

Asterisk

The asterisk (°) means that you must repeat the instructions following the asterisk as many times as specified. Whenever an asterisk is used in a pattern, you will find an ending asterisk also. The sequence of the pattern is repeated between the asterisks.

> *Example*: Ch 2, ° sk 2 sts, sc in next st, sk 2 sts, 2 dc in next st, ch 1, 2 dc in same st, repeat from ° 3 times.

In doing this work, you would chain two (notice the asterisk); then skip two stitches, single crochet in next stitch . . . to end of asterisk; then repeat the work between the asterisks three *more* times. Altogether you should do the work between the asterisks four times.

Double Asterisks

Oftentimes double asterisks (°°) and single asterisks are given in the same pattern. In a case such as this, the writer may want part of the pattern repeated several times; then the entire pattern repeated several times. This can present a problem to a person who is not familiar with reading patterns with double and single asterisks.

> *Example*: "Dc in dc, °° ch 9, 1 dc in each of the 1st 3 dc, ° ch 1, sk 1 dc, 1 dc in each of the next 3 dc, repeat from ° 2 times, repeat from °° to end of row, ch 4, turn.

If you were reading and doing this work, you would start out with one double crochet stitch in the double crochet stitch of the previous row (notice the double asterisks), chain nine, work one double crochet stitch in each of the first three double crochet stitches, (notice the single asterisks), chain one, skip one double crochet stitch, make a double crochet stitch in each of the next three double crochet stitches. Then you would repeat the work from the single asterisk two times *more*. Start again at the double asterisks (chain nine, and so on), repeating thus to the end of the row.

Dagger

A dagger (†) is used in the same manner as the asterisk as explained above.

Parentheses

You may be given instructions that have parentheses ( ) as well as asterisks and daggers. When parentheses are used, you must do the work between the parentheses as many times as specified.

Example: (Ch 4, sk next 3ch, dc in next ch) 3 times.

The work between the parentheses is to be done *three* times before you read and work further through the pattern.

Note: The use of parentheses differs from the use of asterisks and daggers in that you do not do the work and then repeat for the specified number of times. You simply do the work as many times (in all) as stated after the closing parenthesis mark.

EXPLANATION OF DIFFERENT PATTERN STITCHES

Many times a pattern maker will refer to a certain part of the pattern stitch as a shell, a cluster, a popcorn, etc. There are many ways of making such stitches. The instructions will tell exactly how to make them. They will state, for example, ". . . a cluster stitch made." The next time you are to make a cluster, step-by-step insructions will not be given; they will simply say, "Make a cluster in next stitch."

Example: Holding back last lp of each dc, work 2 dc in next st, yo and pull yarn through 3 lps on hook (cluster dc or cl-dc made), * ch 1, sk next ch, cl-dc in next ch.

In the above example, the cluster double crochet stitch is made by holding back the last loop on each double crochet stitch, yarning over and pulling a loop through three loops on the hook.

Example of a shell stitch: Sc in 2nd ch from hook, * sk next 2 ch, ch 1, work shell of (dc, ch 1) 3 times in next ch, sk next 2 ch, sc in next ch, repeat from * across.

In the above example, the writer wants you to work a shell of one double crochet stitch, chain one, one double crochet stitch, chain one, one double crochet stitch, chain one, all in the next chain stitch.

Another example of a shell stitch: * sk 2 ch, 5 dc in next ch (shell), sk 2 ch, sc in next ch; rep from *.

In the above pattern, a shell is made by making five double crochet stitches in one chain stitch.

All instructions are telling you where to place the stitches on the row you have just finished. For example, if the pattern reads, "ch 3, turn, 1 dc in 2nd st and in each st across row," you will chain three at the end of the row; then turn your work around and start working the next row by placing a double crochet stitch in the second stitch (of the row you just finished) and in each stitch across the row.

Occasionally, you may be given directions to place a stitch on top of some stitches that you are working on the same row, and not in the row below.

Example: Tr in next st, ch 3, hdc in tr just made, tr in next st.

To do this, place a treble crochet stitch in the next stitch (on the row below), chain three, place a half double crochet stitch

on the *tip* of the treble you just made; then place a treble
crochet stitch in the next stitch (on the row below).

You must always place your stitches in the complete stitch of
the previous row. If the pattern does not want you to do this, the
pattern will state, for example, "working through back loops only,
place 1 dc st in each st." When you work stitches in the back loop
only, a ridge is left on the side facing you. Sometimes a pattern
maker will wish to create this effect, or the pattern maker may
wish you to place stitches in the front loop only.

> *Example*: Working in front loop only, place 1 sc in each
> st across now.

This causes a ridge on the opposite side of the work. Remember, if nothing is said about front or back loops, the pattern
maker wishes you to place all stitches through the complete
stitch (both loops).

New crocheters may become confused when told to place
stitches in a space or spaces.

> *Example*: Row 1: * dc in next dc, ch 3, sk next 3 sts,
> repeat from * across row, ending 1 dc in last dc, ch 3
> turn.
> Row 2: * 3 dc in next space, 1 dc in next dc, repeat
> from * across row.

Explanation: Work row 1, placing one double crochet stitch in
the double crochet stitch of the previous row, chain three, skip
the next three double crochet stitches of the previous row. Double
crochet stitch in the next double crochet stitch of the previous
row, etc., repeating between the asterisks until you come to the
end of the row and ending by placing a double crochet stitch in

the last double crochet stitch. Chain three and turn your work around.

Work row 2 by placing three double crochet stitches in the complete space of the chain three of the previous row; then one double crochet stitch in the next double crochet stitch, etc.

If the pattern maker wanted you to place the double crochet stitches in each of the chains of the chain three of the previous row, she would not have said to place the stitches in the "chain three space." The pattern would then have read, "1 dc in next dc, 1 dc in each of the next 3 ch."

Reading some patterns can be quite distressing. All pattern makers write differently, and if you read and work with many different patterns, you will gradually become accustomed to the ways in which most pattern makers word their instructions. Build your knowledge gradually, starting with comparatively easy instructions, and then work your way up to harder and more difficult patterns.

Japanese people are very artistic, very creative, and excellent needleworkers. The Japanese crochet patterns are all worked out with symbols instead of words. Their patterns can be read by anyone, as the symbols seem to be an international language which anyone can understand. Various examples of these patterns are given in the chapter called Medallions, page 245.

PATTERN STITCHES

There are many ways of working various pattern stitches, such as shells, popcorns, clusters, stars, etc. Your pattern will give you specific steps to follow to form these stitches. Some examples of these stitches will be discussed and shown on the following pages to familiarize you with the general characteristics of each kind of stitch.

V Stitch

Make a foundation chain.

Row 1: Dc in 5th ch from hook, ch 1, dc in same ch, * sk 2 ch, in next ch work: dc, ch 1 dc (V st), repeat from * end dc in last ch, ch 3, turn.

Row 2: Work V st of dc, ch 1, dc in each ch-1 sp of each V st across, end dc in top of turning ch, ch 3, turn. Repeat row 2.

Explanation: Working back on the foundation chain, work one double crochet stitch in the fifth chain from the hook, chain one, place another double crochet stitch in the same chain, * skip two chains on the foundation chain, then work a V stitch by working one double crochet stitch, chain one, one double crochet stitch *all in the next chain*. Then repeat from the asterisk, skipping two chain stitches on the foundation chain between the V stitches each time; end by skipping two chains, then work a double crochet stitch in the last chain. Chain three and turn.

When working row 2, place a V stitch in each of the chain one *spaces* in the previous row. End by working one double crochet stitch in the top of the turning chain.

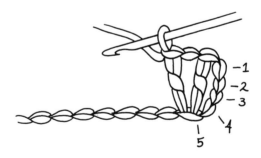

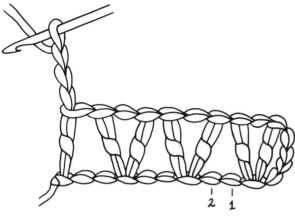

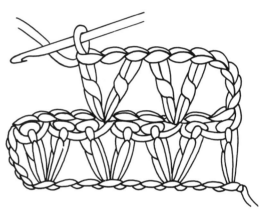

"V" Stitch

Shell and V Stitch

Make a foundation chain of desired length.

Row 1: 1 dc in 5th ch from hook, * skip 3 sts, 5 dc in next st (1 shell made) skip 3 sts, 1 dc, ch 2 and 1 dc in next st (1 V st made), repeat from * across row, ch 5, turn.

Row 2: 1 dc in first space, * 1 shell in center dc of next shell, 1 V st in ch-2 sp of next V st, repeat from * across row ending, 1 shell in center dc of next shell, 1 dc, ch 2, and 1 dc in space between last dc and turning ch, ch 5, turn. Repeat row 2 for pattern.

Explanation: Work row 1, placing the first double crochet stitch in the fifth chain from the hook. Skip three chains on the foundation chain; then make a shell of five double crochet stitches *all in the next chain*. Skip three chains on the foundation chain; then make a V stitch of one double crochet stitch, chain two, and one double crochet stitch *all in the next chain*. Continue thus across the row. You must end the row with a V stitch; chain five stitches and turn.

On row 2, place the first double crochet stitch in the first chain-two space (this is counted as the first V stitch). Then place a shell of five double crochet stitches in the *center* double crochet stitch of the shell in the previous row. Place a V stitch consisting of one double crochet stitch, chain two, and one double crochet stitch in the *chain-two space* of the V stitch in the previous row. Continue across the row in this manner, and place the last V stitch in the *space* between the last double crochet stitch and the turning chain (of the previous row).

Shell and "V" Stitch

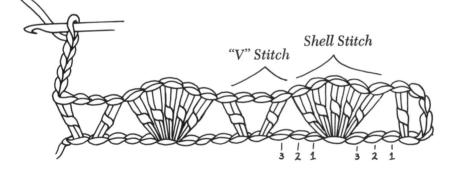

"V" Stitch   Shell Stitch

3 2 1   3 2 1

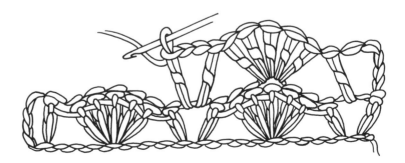

Shell Stitch

Make a foundation chain.

Row 1: Make a half shell of 2 dc in 4th ch from hook, * skip 2 ch, in next ch make 2 dc, ch 2, 2 dc (shell st made) repeat from * ending skip 2 ch, half shell of 2 dc in last ch. Ch 4, turn.

Row 2: Work half shell in first dc, * shell in ch 2 space of next shell, repeat from * across, ending half shell in last dc, ch 4, turn. Repeat row 2 for pattern.

Explanation: Work row 1, starting back on the foundation chain, by placing two double crochet stitches in the fourth chain from the hook, * skip the next two chains on the foundation chain. In the next chain (on the foundation chain), make a shell stitch consisting of two double crochet stitches, chain two stitches, and two double crochet stitches (the stitches of this shell are *all* placed in *one* chain of the foundation chain). Repeat from the * ending skip two chains on the foundation chain, and then work a half shell consisting of two double crochet stitches in the last chain. Chain four and turn your work around.

Work row 2, starting with a half shell of two double crochet stitches placed in the first double crochet stitch of the previous row, * in the chain-two *space* of the next shell (in the previous row), work a shell of two double crochet stitches, chain two and two double crochet stitches. Repeat from the * across the row, ending by placing a half shell, consisting of two double crochet stitches in the last double crochet stitch. Chain four and turn your work around. Repeat the second row for the pattern.

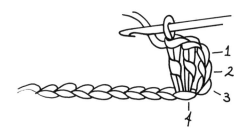

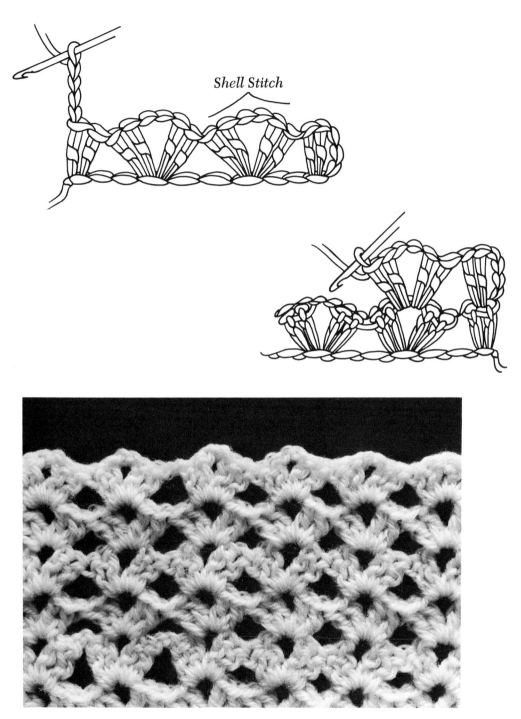

Shell Stitch

Shell Stitch

Staggered Shell Stitch

Make a chain of desired length.

Row 1: 2 dc in 4th ch from hook (half shell) * skip 2 ch, 1 sc in next ch, skip 2 ch, 5 dc in next st (shell) sk 2 ch, sc in next ch, repeat form * ending sk 2 ch, half shell in last ch, ch 1, turn.

Row 2: Sc in 1st st, * shell in next sc, sc in center st of next shell, repeat from * ending shell in next sc, sc in top of turning ch, ch 3, turn.

Row 3: 2 dc in first sc (half shell) * sc in center st of next shell, 1 shell in next sc, repeat from * ending 1 sc in center st of next shell, 2 dc in last sc. Ch 1, turn. Repeat rows 2 and 3 for pattern.

Explanation: A shell is formed by making five double crochet stitches in one stitch. A half shell is made by making two double crochet stitches in one stitch. Working back on the foundation chain of row 1, place two double crochet stitches in the fourth chain from the hook. This forms a half shell on the edge. * Skip two chains on the foundation chain), then place one single crochet stitch in the next chain stitch, skip two more chains (on the foundation chain), and place a shell in the next chain. The shell is made by placing five double crochet stitches *all in the next chain*. Skip two chains (on the foundation chain) and place one single crochet stitch in the next chain. Repeat from the * and end the row by skipping two chains. Place a half shell consisting of two double crochet stitches in the last chain. Chain one and turn.

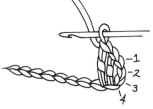

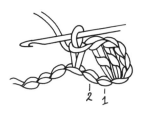

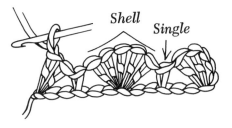

Note: On the first completed row you have formed one half shell on each end of the piece. The rest of the row consists of full shells.

Row 2 starts by placing one single crochet stitch in the first double crochet stitch (of the previous row). * Then a shell consisting of five double crochet stitches is placed in the next single crochet stitch. Place a single crochet stitch in the *center stitch* of the next shell stitch (of the previous row). Repeat from the * and end by placing a shell stitch in the next single crochet stitch; then place a single crochet stitch in the top of the turning chain. Chain three and turn the work around.

Note: On the second row you do not work any half shells. The row starts and ends with full shells.

Row 3 is worked by placing a half shell in the first single crochet stitch; then a single crochet stitch is placed in the center stitch of the next shell stitch. A full shell is placed in the next single crochet stitch; a single crochet stitch is placed in the center stitch of the next shell. This staggers the shells and the row ends with a half shell. Rows 2 and 3 are repeated for the pattern.

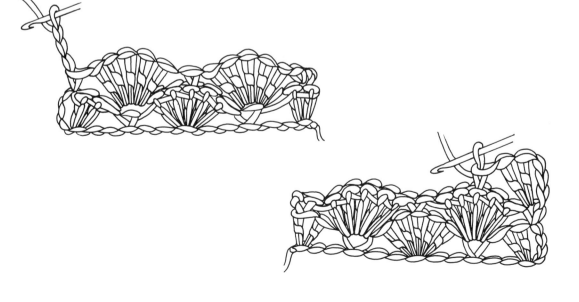

Staggered Shell Stitch

Slant Shell Stitch

Make a chain of desired length.

Row 1: Work 2 dc in 4th st from hook, sk 3 sts, sl st in next st * ch 3, 2 dc in same st with sl st, sk 3 sts, sl st in next st. Repeat from * across row, ch 3, turn.

Row 2: Work 2 dc in sl st, sl st in ch-3 loop of shell of previous row, * ch 3, 2 dc in same sp, sl st in next ch-3 lp, repeat from * across row, ch 3, turn. Repeat row two for pattern.

Explanation: After the chain of desired length has been worked, start row 1 by working two double crochet stitches in the fourth chain from the hook, skip the next three stitches, slip stitch in the

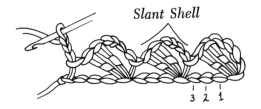

Slant Shell

next stitch, chain three stitches, place two double crochet stitches in the *same place* where the slipped stitch was placed, skip three stitches, slip stitches in the next stitch; then repeat from the asterisk across the row. You will be ending with a slip stitch. Chain three and turn.

Start the next row by working two double crochet stitches in the slip stitch at the end of the previous row; then slip stitch in the chain-three loop of the next shell, chain three, work two double crochet stitches in the same chain-three loop, slip stitch in the chain-three loop of the next shell, repeating across the row and ending with a slip stitch in the last chain-three loop, chain three and turn. Make sure that you maintain the same number of shells on each row. (See photograph.)

Slant Shell Stitch

Picot Stitch

Work a foundation chain.

Work 1 sc in 2nd ch from hook, * ch 3, sl st in top of sc just made (picot stitch), sc in next 4 sts, picot, repeat from * across row.

Explanation: A picot stitch can be worked on top of any kind of stitch simply by slip stitching in the tip of the stitch just before the chain three. Often the pattern will require a different number of chain stitches, depending upon how large a picot is required.

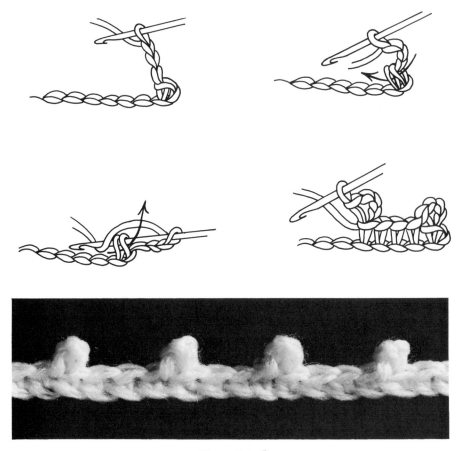

Picot Stitch

Popcorn Stitch

Work a foundation chain.

Row 1: Work 5 dc in the 6th ch from hook; drop loop from hook; insert hook in the top of 1st dc on the group of 5 just made; insert it also in dropped loop and draw the loop through, ch 1 to secure (a popcorn), * ch 1, sk next st, 1 dc in next st, ch 2, sk next st, a popcorn in next st; repeat from * across, ch 3, turn.

Row 2: * 1 dc in pc, 1 dc in next ch-2 sp, 1 dc in next dc, 1 dc in ch-2 sp; repeat from * end 1 dc in pc, 1 dc in turning ch, ch 4, turn. Repeat these 2 rows for pattern.

Explanation: After the foundation chain has been worked, work five double crochet stitches in the sixth chain from the hook. Pull up a long loop and then remove the hook from the loop. Insert the hook in the tip of the first double crochet stitch you made. Take up the long loop left at the end of the five double crochet stitches and pull the long loop through, tighten the loop, then chain one stitch to secure popcorn, chain one, skip the next stitch, place one double crochet stitch in the next stitch, chain

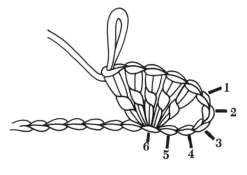
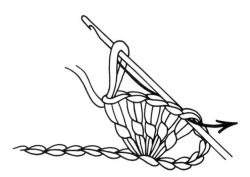

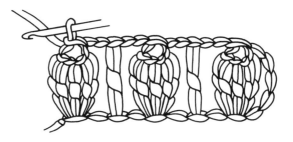

two stitches, skip the next stitch, and work another popcorn in the next stitch as before. Work second row.

Note: All five double crochet stitches which will form the popcorn have been worked in one stitch.

The pattern quoted has one double crochet post stitch between popcorns. Other popcorn patterns may not have anything in between the popcorns. In that case, you may be required to work several chain stitches between popcorns. (See photograph.)

Popcorn Stitch

Cluster Stitch

Work a foundation chain.

Row 1: * Holding back last lp of each dc, work 3 dc in 5th ch from hook, yo and pull lp through 4 lps on hook, ch 1 to secure (cluster st), ch 1, sk next 2 ch, work a cl in next st. Repeat from * across, ch 3, turn.

Row 2: * Work a cl st in next sp, ch 2; repeat from * across row, end 1 cl in turning ch. Repeat rows 1 and 2 for pattern.

Explanation: Working back on the foundation chain, work a cluster stitch by working three double crochet stitches in the fifth chain from the hook, always retaining the last loop of each double crochet stitch on the hook; yarn over and pull a loop through all four loops on the hook and chain one to secure cluster. Cluster stitch completed. * Chain one, skip two stitches, and work another cluster stitch in the next stitch. Repeat from the asterisk to the end of the row. On row 2, work cluster stitches in the chain-two spaces.

Note: Cluster stitches may be made with treble crochet stitches instead of double crochet stitches, depending upon the requirements of the pattern maker. A tight chain stitch should be made after drawing the loop through all four loops on the hook to hold the cluster tightly together.

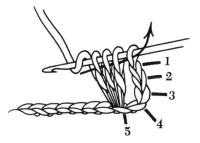
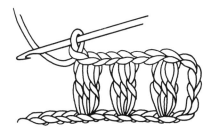

Cluster Stitch

Puff Stitch

Puff Stitch

Work a foundation chain of approximately twenty chains.

Row 1: Work 1 row of single crochet stitches across foundation chain, ch 6, turn.

Row 2: Yo hook, sk 1 sc, insert hook in next sc, pull up a lp ½" high, (yo hook, insert hook in same sc, pull up a lp to same height) twice, yo hook and through 7 lps on hook, ch 1 (puff st made), * ch 2, sk 2 sc, puff st in next st. Repeat from * across row, ch 1, turn.

Row 3: Sc in each puff st and each ch across row. Ch 4, turn. Repeat rows 2 and 3 for pattern.

Explanation: After you have worked the foundation row and the row of single crochet stitches, chain six stitches; then work the first puff stitch by working in the second single crochet stitch. Yarn over hook, pull up a loop one-half inch high, yarn over, pull up another loop one-half inch high in the same stitch, yarn over, and pull up another loop in the same stitch one-half inch high. You now have seven loops on the hook and all loops were worked in the same single crochet stitch in the row below. Yarn over once more and pull a loop through all seven loops on the hook. Chain one to secure the puff stitch; then chain two, skip two single crochet stitches in the previous row, and place a puff stitch in the next single crochet stitch. When you reach the end of the row, chain one and turn.

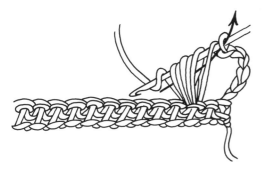
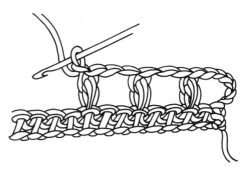

Cross Puff Stitch

Work a foundation chain.

Row 1: Work a row of single crochet stitches, chain 3, turn.

Row 2: * Sk 1 sc, yo hook, insert hook in next sc, pull up a lp ½″ high, (yo, insert hook in same sc, pull up a lp to same height) twice, yo and through 7 lps on hook, ch 1 (1 puff stitch made); working over first puff st (yo hook, insert hook in skipped sc, pull up a lp ½″ high) 3 times, yo hook, and through 7 lps on hook, ch 1 (cross puff st made); repeat from * to end, ch 1, turn.

Row 3: Sc in each puff st across row. Repeat rows 2 and 3 for pattern.

Explanation: This cross puff stitch is made like the puff stitch previously explained. The first puff stitch is placed in the second single crochet stitch; then another puff stitch is placed in the first single crochet stitch which was just skipped. After you chain one to secure the puff stitch, there are no other chains in between the puff stitches. (See photograph.)

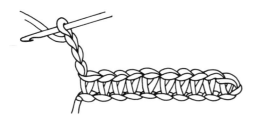

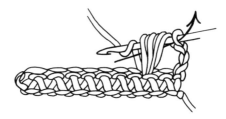

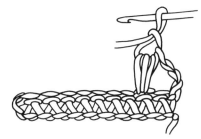

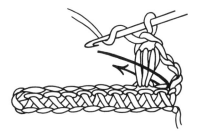

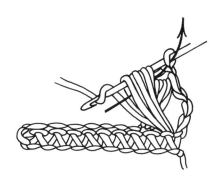

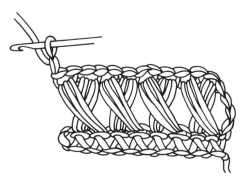

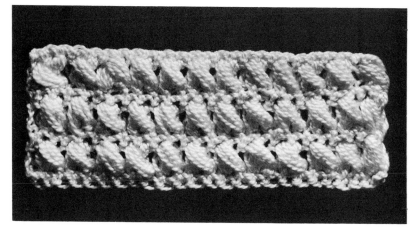

Cross Puff Stitch

Star Stitch

Make a foundation chain.

Row 1: Draw up a lp in 2nd ch from hook and in each of next 3 ch, yo and through 5 lps on hook, ch 1 for *eye* (star st made). *Draw up a lp in *eye* just made, then in same ch last worked and in each of next 2 ch, yo and through 5 lps on hook, ch 1 for *eye* (star st), repeat from * across, ch 2 and turn.

Row 2: The ch 2 (counts as 1 hdc), hdc in first *eye* (1 pat), * 2 hdc in next *eye* (1 pat) repeat from * across, end 1 hdc in top of turning ch, ch 3, turn.

Row 3: Draw up a lp in 2nd and 3rd ch from hook, sk first hdc, draw up a lp in each of next 2 hdc, yo and through 5 lps on hook, ch 1 for *eye* (star st), * draw up a lp˙ in *eye* just made, then in same hdc last worked and in each of next 2 hdc, yo and through 5 lps on hook, ch 1 for *eye*, repeat from * across, end last hdc of last repeat in top of turning ch, ch 2, turn. Repeat rows 2 and 3 for pat.

Explanation: This stitch is a little hard to do because it is not easy to see the *eye* of the star from the wrong side when you are working the second row. Count the number of star stitches you are working with on your sample so that you can maintain the same number of star stitches across all rows.

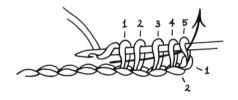

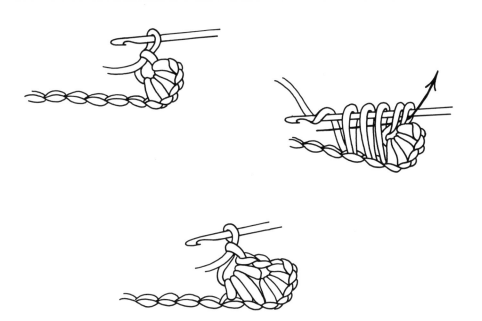

Starting back on your foundation chain and working row 1, draw up a loop in the second chain from the hook and in each of the next three chain stitches (five loops on hook), yarn over and through five loops on the hook, and chain one for the *eye*. This is the first star stitch. * Draw up a loop in the *eye* just made (you must insert the hook into the little thread which is a single loop in back of the chain one just made), then another loop in the same foundation chain last worked for the last star stitch made, then loops in each of the next two foundation chains (five loops on hook), yarn over and through five loops on hook and chain one for *eye* (star stitch completed). Repeat from the asterisk across the row and turn.

For row 2, chain two (the chain two counts as the first half double crochet stitch), and place one half double crochet stitch in the first *eye*. You may have to look to the opposite side of your work to find the hole of the *eye* stitch in the previous row. This is the first pattern completed. * Work two half double crochet

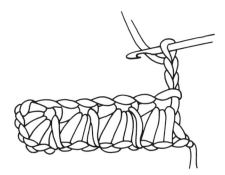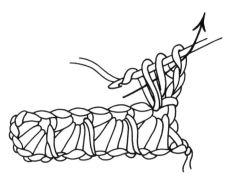

stitches in the next *eye* (another pattern completed), repeat from the asterisk across the row, and end by placing one half double crochet stitch on top of the turning chain and turn.

For row 3, chain three. Next, draw up a loop in the second chain from the hook, draw up another loop in the third chain from the hook; now skip the first half double crochet stitch of the previous row. Draw up a loop in each of the next two half double crochet stitches (five loops on the hook), yarn over and pull a loop through all five loops on the hook. Chain one for the *eye* (first star stitch completed), * draw up a loop in the *eye* just made (you must insert the hook into the little thread which is a single loop in back of the chain one just made), and then draw up a loop in the same half double crochet stitch last worked and draw up loops in each of the next two half double crochet stitches (five loops on the hook). Yarn over and pull the loop through all

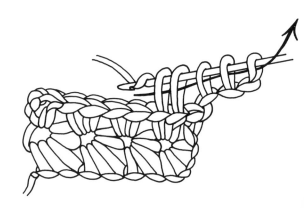

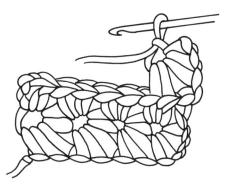

five loops on the hook, chain one for the *eye*, and repeat from the asterisk across the row. The last half double crochet stitch of the last repeat is placed on top of the turning chain of the previous row. Turn. Repeat rows 2 and 3 for the pattern.

Note: On row 1, which is a right-side row, the star stitch is started with all of the little threads stretching out from the *eye*. On the second row, which is the wrong-side row, the pattern is completed by working the half double crochet stitches. Row 3 is practically a repeat of the first row, with the exception that all stitches on the first row are placed in the foundation chain and are not placed through the half double crochet stitches you worked for row 2. (See photographs.)

Star Stitch

Knot Stitch (Lover's Knot Stitch)

Work a foundation chain for desired length.

Row 1: Sc in 2nd ch from hook, * draw up a lp ¾″ long, yo and draw lp through long lp; 1 sc in single strand of long lp (knot st made), work another knot stitch, sk 4 ch, sc in next ch, repeat from * across row.

Row 2: Turn, * work 3 knot sts, sc in first lp of next double knot st (to right of knot), sc in 2nd lp of same knot st (to left of same knot), make a double knot st, repeat from * across. Repeat row 2.

Explanation: This stitch is very lacy and delicate. It works up quite rapidly once the stitch has been mastered.

Starting back on the foundation chain and working row 1, place a single crochet stitch in the second chain from the hook. * Now draw up a loop on the hook approximately three-fourths of an inch long, and draw a loop through. Notice that there is a single thread to the left of the hook and to the left of the chain loop which is on the hook. Place one single crochet stitch through that single thread. You have just formed one knot stitch. Now,

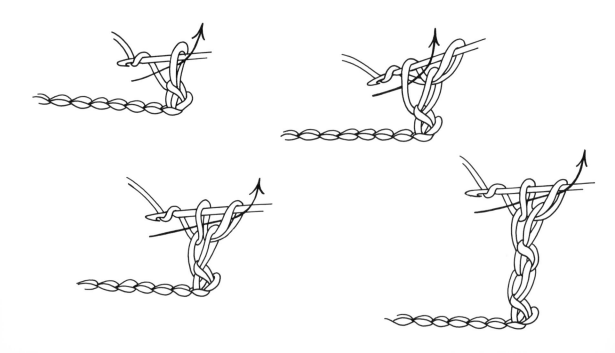

Lover's Knot Stitch

work another knot stitch in the same manner (double knot stitch made). Skip four chains on the foundation row, single crochet in the next chain, and repeat from the asterisk across the row.

For row 2, turn your work around to work back over the first row of double knot stitches. Start the row by working three knot stitches to raise to the level of the second row. Next, * place a single crochet stitch in the first long loop of the double knot stitch in the previous row. This stitch is placed to the *right* of the "knot." Now, place another single crochet stitch in the next long loop. This stitch is placed to the *left* of the same knot. (See drawings.) Work a double knot stitch; then repeat from the asterisk to the end of the row. Row 2 is repeated over and over for the desired number of rows. (See photograph.)

Loop Stitch

Work a foundation chain.

Row 1: Sc in 2nd ch from hook and in each ch across row. Ch 1, turn.

Row 2: 1 lp st in each sc (wind yarn over index finger, insert hook in st, draw yarn through pulling yarn from under finger, drop loop from finger, letting loops fall to right side of work, and complete sc), ch 1, turn.

Row 3: Sk 1st st, 1 sc in each st across row. Ch 1, turn.
Repeat rows 2 and 3 for pattern.

Explanation: Work the foundation chain and the row of single crochet stitches. Chain one and turn.

Start row 2, *which is a wrong-side row*. *Wrap the yarn around the index finger of your left hand (see drawing). Hold the index finger very close to the top of the row. Now place the hook into the next single crochet stitch of the previous row and draw up a

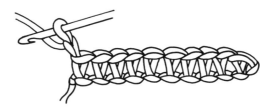

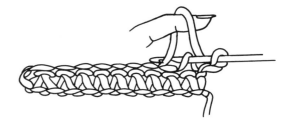

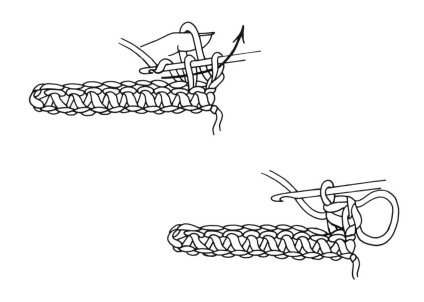

loop on the hook. Remove the index finger of your left hand from the long loop and finish the single crochet stitch (see drawing). Repeat from the asterisk to the end of the row.

Note: Observe that all loops which were formed by placing the yarn over your left index finger are falling to the *right side* of your work. Chain one and turn work around.

For row 3 (right side of work), skip the first stitch and work one single crochet stitch in each single crochet stitch across the row. Chain one and turn your work around. Repeat rows 2 and 3 for the pattern.

Loop Stitch

Double Loop Stitch

The double loop stitch is worked the same way as the single loop stitch, with the following exception: The yarn is wrapped around the index finger of the left hand twice instead of once. When the loops are dropped off the finger, the result is a loop twice as long—not two separate loops.

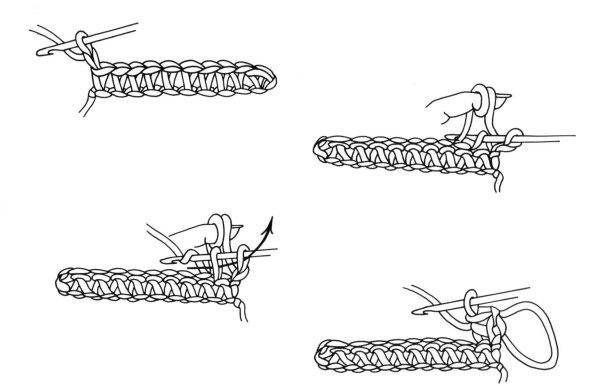

Roll Stitch

Work a foundation chain for desired length.

Work a roll st in 6th ch from hook and in each ch across row. To work roll st—yo hook 16 times, insert hook into ch, draw up loop, yo and draw through coil, ch 1 to secure coil.

Explanation: The roll stitch is a very old stitch, dating back to the early 1840s. See page 258, showing a medallion using this lovely old stitch.

After the foundation chain has been worked, yarn over the hook sixteen times; then place the hook into the sixth chain from the hook and draw a loop through. Yarn over hook and pull the loop through all the loops on the hook (the coil). It is a little difficult to pull the hook through the coil without catching the hook in some of the threads of the coil. Therefore, it is best to open up the coil by pushing the coil onto the shank part of the hook to make uniform the threads which comprise the coil. Next, grasp the coil and hold it together with the fingers of your left hand; point the hook down and carefully draw the hook through the coil. The roll stitch when completed, is straight with a thread the

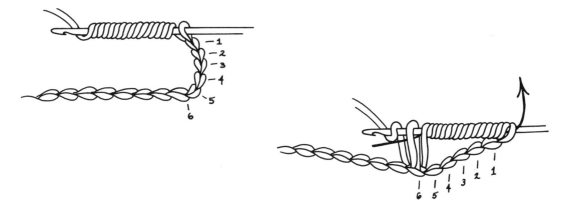

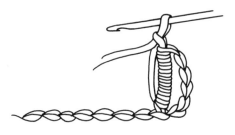

length of the roll on its left side. (See drawing.) Chain one to secure the roll. Work another roll stitch, etc. across the row.

There are other variations of the roll stitch. For example, if the thread to the left of the coil is drawn tighter, the roll stitch will become curved. The thread to the left of the stitch may even be pulled so tight that it will bend the coil nearly half to the work. (See photograph.) The length of the rolls may be regulated by the number of times the thread or yarn is thrown over the hook. The fewer times it is thrown over, the easier it is to pull the hook through the coil; however, the longer rolls with more wraps over the hook are much prettier and they can be drawn into tighter curved rolls than those with fewer wraps over the hook.

Roll Stitch

Around-the-Post Stitch

Work a foundation chain and one row of double crochet stitches across the chain, chain three, turn work around.

Work a dc around the post of the second dc, * dc in next dc, dc around the post of next dc; repeat from * across row, ch 3, turn.

Explanation: After the foundation chain and a row of double crochet stitches have been worked for the first row, chain three and turn the work around. The instructions read to work a double crochet stitch around the post of the next double crochet stitch. If you are to work the double crochet stitch around the post from the back side, the instructions will tell you to do so. In most instructions, however, if you are not given the direction of the around-the-post stitch, you should assume the writer means that you are to go around the post of the next stitch from the front:

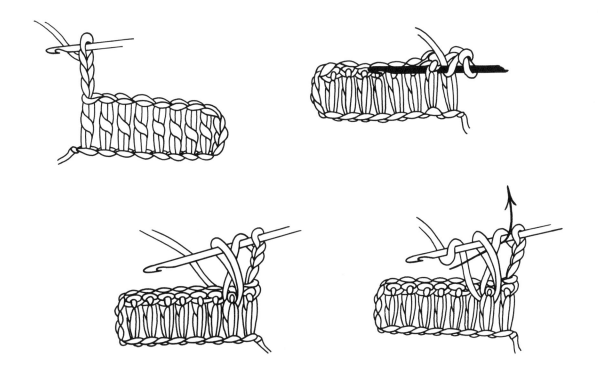

Yarn over hook, insert hook from the front of the work to the back and around the body or post of the next double crochet stitch of the previous row; thus bringing the hook back into position on the front side of your work (the side facing you). Yarn over and pull a loop through, yarn over through two loops, yarn over and pull through the last two loops on the hook. This gives a lovely raised stitch on the right side of your work. If the pattern maker wishes you to place around-the-post stitches on the next row, you will need to work around the post back: Yarn over the hook and insert the hook from the *back to the front of work* and around the body or post of the next double crochet stitch of the previous row. The hook is now in the position at the back of your work. Yarn over and pull loop through, yarn over through two loops, and yarn over and pull the loop through the last two loops on the hook (see photograph). Single crochet stitches around-the-post may be made in the same manner, either from the front or from the back.

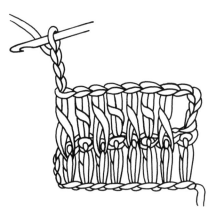

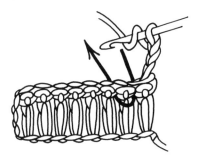

Around-The-Post Stitch

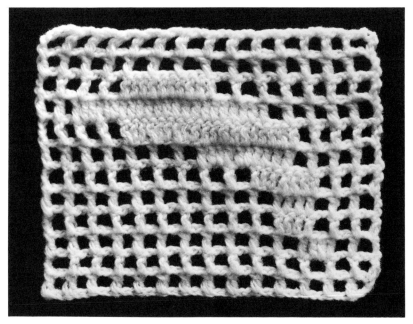

Filet Crochet Stitch

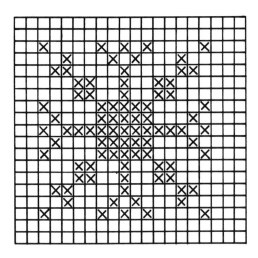

Filet Crochet

Filet crochet is formed by blocks and spaces. Usually the double crochet stitch is used throughout. The open mesh is referred to as "the space."

If you are following a pattern in a book, using filet crochet, you will be given a chart that shows the squares in open mesh and solid blocks. (See example chart.)

Work a chain for desired length.

Row 1: To form the first row of open mesh, work the first double crochet stitch in the eighth chain from the hook, * chain two, skip two chains, one double crochet stitch in the next chain, repeat from the asterisk to the end of the row. Chain five and turn.

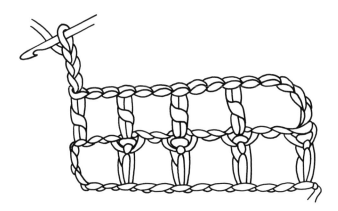

Row 2: One double crochet stitch in the second double
crochet stitch of the previous row, * chain two, one
double crochet stitch in the next double crochet stitch of
the previous row; repeat from the asterisk to the end of
the row, placing the last double crochet stitch in the third
chain of the turning chain five of the previous row. (See
drawing.)

To work the solid blocks: Working on the swatch of open mesh
just made, end the last row with chain three instead of chain five
and turn the work around. * Work one double crochet stitch in
each of the next two chain stitches of the previous row, one
double crochet stitch in the next double crochet stitch of the
previous row (one solid block made). To alternate blocks and
spaces, chain two, skip two chain stitches, work one double crochet stitch in next double crochet stitch (one space made); repeat
from the asterisk across the row. (See photograph.)

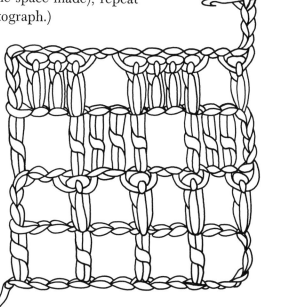

Cross Stitch

> Work a foundation row and one row of single crochet stitches across the foundation chain. Chain three and turn.
>
> *Row 1*: * Sk 1 sc, 1 dc in next sc, 1 dc in skipped sc (cross st made) repeat from * ending 1 dc in last st, ch 1, turn.
>
> *Row 2*: Work 1 sc in each st across row to end, 1 sc in top of turning ch, ch 3, turn. Repeat rows 1 and 2.

Explanation: After the foundation chain has been worked, work one row of single crochet stitches in each chain across the row.

To work row 1, which is the right side of the work, turn the work around and chain three stitches. Skip the first single crochet stitch of the previous row, make a double crochet stitch in the next stitch. Now, make a double crochet stitch in the skipped stitch. One cross stitch has been completed. Continue across the row, skipping the next single crochet stitch of the previous row, placing a double crochet stitch in the next stitch. Make a double crochet stitch in the stitch you skipped (another cross stitch made). Continue in this manner to the end of the row, and then place one double crochet stitch in the top of the turning chain of the previous row. Chain one and turn the work around.

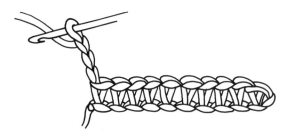

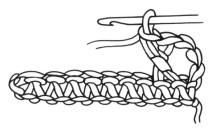

Work row 2 with a single crochet stitch in each stitch across the row, ending with one single crochet on top of the turning chain of the previous row. Be sure to maintain the correct number of stitches on each row.

Note: Review page 16 before starting row 1. The chain-three at the beginning of the row counts as the first double crochet stitch for this row, and it is on top of the last single crochet stitch of the previous row. If you are to skip a stitch, place a double crochet stitch in the next stitch; it will look as though you are skipping *two* stitches. You are actually skipping only one stitch, because the first stitch already has a stitch over it—namely, the turning chain. (See photograph.)

Cross Stitch

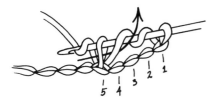

Cross Treble Crochet Stitch

Work a foundation chain for desired length.

Row 1: Yo twice, place hook in 5th ch from hook, *
work off 2 lps, yo, sk 2 sts, place hook in next ch and work
off all lps on hook 2 at a time, ch 2, dc in center to complete cross st. Yo twice, insert hook into next ch, repeat
from *. After last cross st is made, end 1 tr in last ch, ch
4, turn.

Row 2: Work a cross tr on top of each cross tr of previous row.

Explanation: Working back over the foundation chain, yarn
over the hook two times; then place the hook in the fifth chain
from the hook and draw up a loop (four loops on hook). Yarn
over and pull a loop through two loops (three loops left on the
hook); yarn over, skip two chains on the foundation chain, place
the hook into the next chain and pull up a loop (five loops on
hook). Yarn over and pull through two loops (four loops on hook),
yarn over and pull loop through two loops (three loops left on
hook). Yarn over and pull loop through two loops (two loops left
on hook), yarn over and pull loop through the last two loops. At
this point, one-half of the cross stitch has been made. Now,
chain two stitches; then work one double crochet stitch in the
center of the cross to complete the cross (see drawing). The next
cross treble crochet stitch is formed, starting in the next chain of
your foundation chain. Work across the foundation chain, making

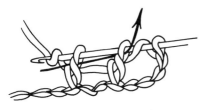

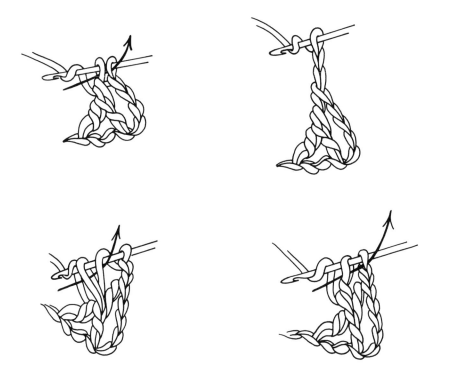

cross treble crochet stitches until the last chain stitch. Work one treble crochet stitch in the last chain. Chain four and turn the work around.

Start the second row, forming the first cross treble crochet stitch on top of the last cross treble crochet stitch of the previous row, and work a cross treble crochet stitch on top of each of the cross treble crochet stitches to the end of the row. Then place a treble crochet stitch on top of the turning chain of the row below (see photograph).

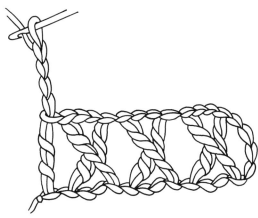

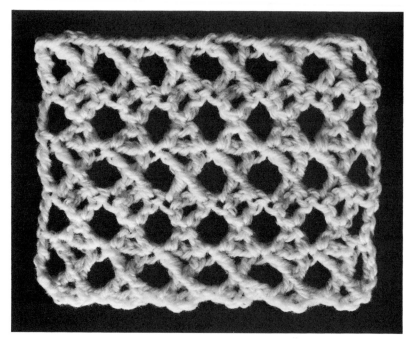

Cross Treble Crochet Stitch

Crocheting Colored Designs

If your pattern requires two or more colors to be used throughout, you may use either of the methods described below:

1. The color not in use should be carried loosely across the wrong side of the work, and then taken up again when needed.

2. The color not in use should be carried across the top of the row just worked, and it will be covered as it is encased in the base of the new stitches of the second color.

Regardless of which method you use, you will change colors in the same manner. When it is time to change colors, work until the last stitch of the first color. Still using the first color, work the last stitch to the very last step of that stitch; then, take the first color to the left direction, and bring the new color into position. Work the last step of *that* stitch with the new color.

If you are working from a graph, the graph is read from the bottom to the top. On right-side rows, you must read from right to left, and on wrong-side rows, you must read from left to right. (See sample graph.) This little pattern in two colors would make a pretty belt. See page 253, sample granny square #2, in which two colors are used for every round except the beginning rounds. This sample was made using the second method of changing colors, in which the color not in use was carried across the top of the stitches in the round last worked, and then brought into position when needed.

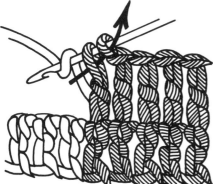

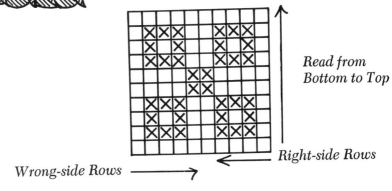

Read from Bottom to Top

Wrong-side Rows ⟶

Right-side Rows

5 Jackets

General

How to Adapt the Jacket Pattern to Fit Your Figure

Crocheting the Jacket
Crocheting the back piece
Crocheting the fronts
Pockets
Positioning of pockets
Other pieces of the jacket

Finishing the Jacket

Jacket with Raglan Sleeves

Double-Breasted Jacket

5 Jackets

GENERAL

Make sure you have read "Conquering Fitting Problems" and "Choosing the Correct Size," pages 32–36. Your personal body measurements must be carefully taken before you start a jacket. *Your jacket will fit only as well as the measurements you have taken.* Your measurements must be taken *over* the heaviest blouse or dress you will ever wear under the jacket. Have someone take these measurements for you. Stand in front of a full-length mirror. Tie a ribbon or a tape around your waist. The second person should measure your bust, waist, and the bottom edge where your jacket will end. The shoulders should be measured from shoulder bone to shoulder bone.

Note: When the bust measurement is taken, the tape should be in line with the fullest part of your bust. Make sure that the tape measure is not sagging in the back. If the tape measure is not on the same horizontal line across your back, you will not get an accurate bust measurement.

Now measure the distances from the nape of your neck to your waist, and from the nape of your neck to the bottom of the jacket. See Drawing 1, showing an example of actual body measurements. The next step is to make a drawing showing your crochet measurements. You must allow approximately three inches at the bust and approximately one inch at the bottom edge. Allow ap-

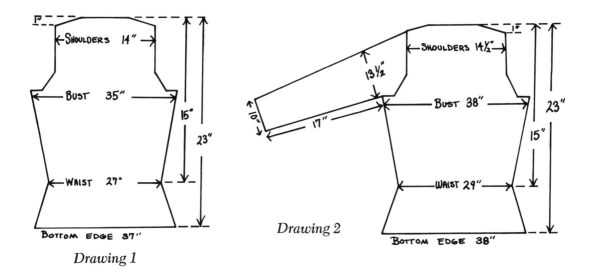

Drawing 1

Drawing 2

proximately one-half inch at the shoulders. See Drawing 2, showing the allowances taken for the example measurements in Drawing 1. You must work from the measurements of Drawing 2. On Drawing 2, you will notice that sleeve lengths have been inserted. To measure your sleeve length, the tape measure should be held approximately two and one-half inches below the point where your arm and body join, measuring from that point to the wrist bone or to whatever length you decide upon. Jacket lengths should be measured from this same point. (See drawings.) Next,

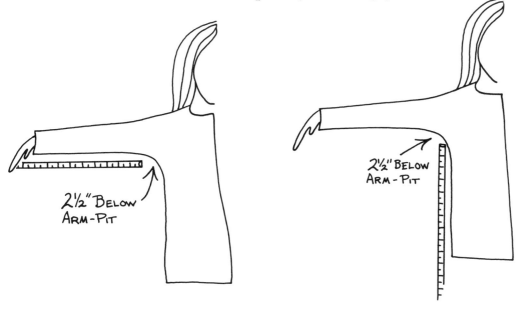

hold the tape loosely around your wrist, adjusting the tape until you feel that the bottom edge of your sleeve is neither too tight nor too loose. This measurement may vary with the type of jacket you intend to make. Your upper-arm measurement should be taken in the same way, that is, with the tape measure held loosely around your upper arm until you feel that there is enough allowance so that the sleeve will not be constricting.

Note: A good guide line to go by for the width at the upper arm is approximately thirteen and one-half to fourteen inches for a small size, fourteen and one-half inches for a medium size, and fifteen inches for a large size.

Most jackets are straight, with no shaping through the waist. However, it is best to include the waist measurements on your drawing of body measurements (Drawing 1) because that measurement enables you to get a correct length measurement from the nape of your neck to the bottom edge of the jacket. Notice that approximately one inch is allowed from the nape of the neck to the place where the shoulder shaping *starts*. This is always shown on the measurement drawings.

HOW TO ADAPT THE JACKET PATTERN TO FIT YOUR FIGURE

Before you can adapt a pattern from a book to your own measurements, you must first diagram the pattern as it is given in the pattern book. When choosing the size from which you will work, take the size closest to your needed bust measurements. (This is not your actual bust measurement—it is your bust measurement plus the needed allowance.)

Read carefully through the pattern to find out how many stitches are required just before the underarm shaping of the back of the jacket. Jot down the number of stitches for the back. Now read through the directions for making the fronts. Look for the number of stitches on each front just before the underarm shaping. Add the back stitches and the front stitches together to find out how many stitches are called for at the bustline. You will next need to know if there is any overlap; if so, how many stitches are involved? Or, perhaps your pattern requires borders to be added later. If the pattern does not tell you how much of the right front overlaps the left front, you can find out by reading where buttonholes are to be placed on the right front. The buttonholes will be placed in the *center* of the overlap.

> *Example*: Work buttonholes as follows: Work 3 sc sts, ch 3, sk 3 sc sts, sc in next st. On the following row, work to buttonhole, then work sc sts over each ch 3.

In the above example, the overlap is nine stitches. The buttonhole is marked in the *center* of the overlap. Three stitches are worked before the start of the buttonhole; then a chain of three stitches, to take the place of the three stitches skipped, places the center of the buttonhole on stitch number five; therefore, nine stitches must be counted in all for the overlap.

After you have chosen from your pattern book the size closest to your needed bust measurement, draw diagrams of the back of the jacket, one front, and one sleeve. Notice Drawing 3—the pattern diagrammed directly from the pattern book. Now change stitches into inches at all the key points in the diagram. In order to do this, you will divide the number of stitches by the stitch gauge given in the pattern book. You must now compare that diagram to *your crochet measurements* (Drawing 2), and make the necessary adjustments to conform to your measurements. Be sure to check on the measurements at this time: the length of the jacket and the sleeve length, and also the width of the sleeves and the cuff measurement.

Caution! Do not try to adjust Drawing 3 to your measurements directly on the same diagram. It is much less confusing if you

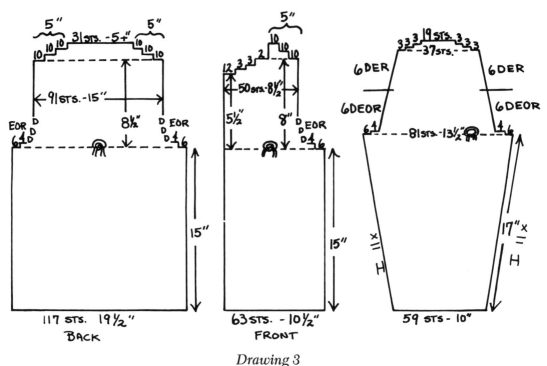

Drawing 3

Gauge 6 sc equals 1″
4 rows equals 1″
overlap of 9 sc stitches

draw a whole new diagram to your measurements. See Drawing 4—the adjusted jacket to the measurements of Drawing 2.

Explanation: When reading through the directions for the jacket diagrammed in the pattern book, the closest size to the example measurement is thirty-nine inches (one inch larger than the needed bust measurement). The shoulder measurement on the diagrammed jacket measures fifteen inches instead of the needed fourteen and one-half inches. Study Drawing 4, which shows how the jacket pattern was adjusted to the measurements of Drawing 2. In order to draw this diagram step-by-step, the shape of the jacket was drawn first. Then the new inch measurements were shown (one-half inch smaller at the bottom edge and the bust, and one-half inch less for the shoulders of the back). The front pattern was also adjusted as to inch measurements. Approximately one-fourth inch less was taken at the bottom edge of the

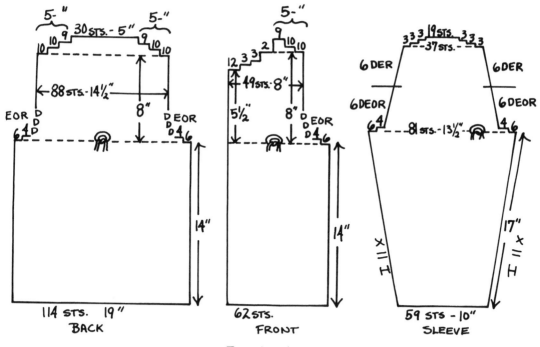

Drawing 4

bust and shoulders. The diagram for the sleeve was not altered because the measurements conformed to the needed sleeve measurements. Finally, the inches were changed into stitches at the proper places on the drawing.

Gauge 6 sc equals 1″
4 rows equals 1″
overlap of 9 sc stitches

CROCHETING THE JACKET

After you have figured out your pattern and diagrams to your own measurements, carefully work your stitch gauge. See page 37 for information on working an accurate stitch gauge. Make a notation of your row and stitch gauge and attach that information to your blocked sample gauge.

Crocheting the Back Piece

Before you commence with the back of the jacket, and assuming that you are working from the diagrams and measurements of the examples used, the bottom edge of the jacket will be wider than needed. There are two ways to correct this discrepancy. You may either start out with fewer stitches and increase up the sides of the jacket, or you may start out with a hook one size smaller. The smaller hook will undoubtedly draw in the bottom edge of the jacket to the needed measurement at that point. There will be some kind of trim on the bottom edge of the jacket, and at that stage of finishing the jacket, you can crochet the edge—holding in the bottom edge to your needed measurement. Try to eliminate increases up the sides if possible; then your jacket will assemble more professionally. Mark the right side (outside) of your work with a scrap of colored yarn. Work on the smaller hook for approximately two to three inches; then use the size hook you decided upon when you worked your stitch gauge. This procedure will give you the necessary shaping at the bottom edge of the jacket. You must also work the front in the same manner: that is, starting out on the smaller hook and changing to the regular hook at the same point as you did on the back of the jacket.

After you have worked for approximately ten inches, stop and block the portion of the back of the jacket. Block the bottom edge to the needed measurement. Then gradually draw the piece out in width until it meets the number of inches you need across the back of the jacket. Next, bring the piece down and up as far as it will stretch, while still maintaining the width measurements that you need at the bottom edge and at the underarm edge. The piece may take a drop of an inch or so, depending upon the yarn you use and how firm your stitch may be. Blocking as you go along will eliminate drastic alterations when the garment is finished.

Note: You need not wash the piece before blocking at this time. You are concerned only with how the piece will stretch in length or draw up in length. Your jacket will be completely washed and blocked when the pieces are finished. The piece will not draw up in length *unless* it is not wide enough. If the piece is too narrow and does not conform to your needed measurements, you will be wise to start again. Obviously you were not maintaining the stitch gauge you decided upon, and some adjustment must be made now, or the garment will not fit. YOU MUST MAINTAIN YOUR STITCH GAUGE.

Let us assume the back piece blocked satisfactorily. When it is dry, begin again. For example, if you were to work for fourteen inches before reaching the underarm, and your blocked piece now measures eleven inches, this means that the piece grew approximately one inch in length. You will need to work for another three inches. Now measure out three inches on your blocked piece to find out how many rows were used to make up three inches. Work that number of rows, and then do the underarm shaping as prescribed in your diagram. After all of the underarm shaping has been completed, stop and block the piece again to the width measurements required, bringing the piece down and up to get all of the lengthwise stretch out of the piece. Make sure that you are maintaining the correct shoulder measurement according to your diagram.

When the piece is dry again, resume your work. If you must go to an eight-inch armhole depth, count to see how many rows that will be measured directly from your piece of blocked work. Work that number of rows and finish off the shoulder shaping. The back of your jacket is now completed. All of the stretch has been taken out as you proceeded.

Crocheting the Fronts

When it is time to work the front, you need not block all the way along as you did for the back piece. Simply count the number of rows or patterns used before the underarm shaping and use the same number of rows or patterns for the front. Shape the underarm as you did for the back and work until you come to the place where the front neck shaping is to be placed. It is a good idea to stop here and block the front piece to make sure that you are making the neck shaping at the correct place. After the piece has been blocked to the width needed and has been compared to the back piece as to length, and the piece of blocked front is dry, stand in front of a mirror and hold the front piece to your body. Decide whether you have stopped at the proper place for the particular neck shaping you desire. If you are satisfied, proceed with the neck shaping and shoulder shaping. If not, make the correction now. Another piece has been completed.

Next, crochet the second front, counting rows to match the first front. If buttonholes are to be worked into the right front, the button markings must be spaced on the completed left front. Instructions may read, for example, "Mark position for five buttons, the first button one inch above starting edge and the last button one-half inch from start of neck shaping."

On the finished left front, mark the position of the first and last buttons with small safety pins. Now measure with your tape the distance from the first to the last markings. If your jacket requires five buttons, you will need four spaces. (You will always need one less space than the number of buttons.) If the distance between the first and last buttons is seventeen inches, your buttons should be marked four and one-fourth inches apart (seventeen inches divided by four spaces). You should then fasten the safety pins four and one-fourth inches apart. (See drawing.)

As you crochet the right side requiring the buttonholes, count the number of rows on the finished piece to the first button marking and work your first buttonhole at that time. Count rows for the placement of all other buttonholes.

If your jacket requires ribbon facings on the front edges, see page 184 for information about how to apply it.

Caution! If you notice any discrepancy in the widths and

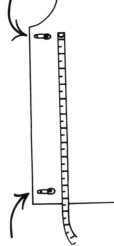

Last Button Marking ½″ from Start of Neck Shaping

First Button Marking 1″ from Bottom Edge

lengths of the two pieces, *you are not maintaining your stitch gauge*. You must not have the front longer than the back, or vice versa. The two pieces must be identical in length. If you were working looser or tighter on one of the pieces, this must be noticed and reworked now, or you will ruin an otherwise beautiful garment. Slow down to maintain the gauge. Careful blocking as you proceed will help eliminate this problem.

POCKETS

Pocket instructions may be included in your pattern. You will probably be given instructions for working the pocket liners first. After you finish the pocket liners, they should be set aside to be used later.

> *Example*: Pocket liners—make 2. Chain 28, work in hdc on 26 sts for 24 rows. Set liners aside. Left front—ch 65 sts. Work in hdc on 63 sts for 6 inches ending at side edge. Next row. Work across 8 sts. Pocket opening—work across 26 sts of pocket liners, skip 26 sts of front piece, work last 29 sts.
>
> (The directions continue on for finishing the left front.)

Explanation: Diagram this left front. All of these instructions should be shown on your diagram. On the row of the pocket opening, you will be working with the right side of the piece facing you and starting at the side edge. Work eight stitches;

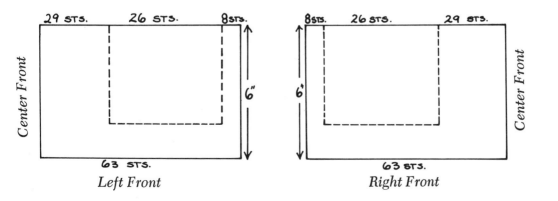

Left Front   Right Front

then work across the twenty-six stitches of one pocket liner; skip twenty-six stitches on the front piece; then work across the last twenty-nine stitches.

The instructions for the right front are not given step by step in most patterns. The pattern may read: "Reverse all shaping and work to correspond to the left front." Make a diagram for the right front as shown. With your diagram in front of you as you are working the right front, you can see that you will be starting the row of the pocket opening from the center front edge instead of from the side edge. You will, therefore, work across twenty-nine stitches, work across the second pocket liner; then work the last eight stitches.

Note: Count rows from the bottom edge of the jacket to the pocket opening to make sure that both pocket openings are being placed on the *same* numbered row.

When you block the fronts with the half-finished pockets, smooth out the pocket liners first; then lay the rest of the front on top of the liners. If another row of crochet or any trim is required on the very top edge of the pocket opening, it should be done after blocking and after assembling. See page 183 for information about tacking the pocket liners in place.

POSITIONING OF POCKETS

Pockets may be worked in the fronts of a jacket whether or not the pattern includes them. All pockets must be placed correctly for your figure. It would be disappointing to find that you had placed the pockets too high or too low after the garment was finished. Pockets are always placed closer to the side seams than the front edges. Look at some of your ready-made garments with pockets; try on one and place your hand in the pocket. Notice where the pockets are located on your body.

After you have crocheted the back of the jacket, fold it in half

and stand in front of a mirror. Hold the half of the back of the
jacket to the front at your left side, as if it were the front. Locate
the exact place where you want your pocket top edge to be
worked and place pins at that location. Now lay the back piece
down flat and count the number of rows from the bottom edge
to the place where the pins were placed. Measure approximately
one and one-half inches in from the side edge and count the
number of stitches; place a pin at that point. Measure across approximately four inches for the pocket width (or a little more if
you wish the opening to be wider). Place a pin at that point. Put
the placement of the pockets directly on your diagram. You will
need to make pocket liners and set them aside to be inserted at
the proper time. The liners will be made with the same number
of stitches you show for the pocket opening, and they can be as
deep as you wish. See page 129 for detailed instructions.

Other Pieces of the Jacket

The sleeves, as were the backs and fronts, should be worked according to your diagram. You should stop short of the sleeve
length needed and block the sleeve piece as you did the back and
the fronts. Careful blocking at this point can eliminate your
having to shorten the sleeves later.

If a collar is to be worked and sewed on, work the collar
according to the directions given in your pattern book.

FINISHING THE JACKET

Now is the time to wash and block all the pieces of your jacket to
the measurements you need. Review "Washing" and "Blocking"
on pages 60–65.

Before assembling the jacket, baste the washed and dried
pieces together and try on the jacket to make sure the fit is

satisfactory. Baste the collar to the neckline. You must know if the cast-on edge (the foundation chain) of the collar is sewed to the neckline or if the outer edge (last row worked) of the collar is sewed to the neckline. Your pattern will state which edge is to be considered the outer or neck edge. In order to set the collar correctly on the neck edge, find the middle of the collar and place a pin at the exact center of the collar. Next, find the center of the back of the neck of the jacket and place a pin at this point. Put the two center pins together. Now read through your pattern book instructions for the finishing details and you will find the place where the collar is to be placed on the front and where the front edge of the collar is to start. Your collar should start at the center of the overlap. If the collar fits at this point, the collar edges will just come together at the front edge when the jacket is buttoned. If there is some trim, such as a row or two of crochet to be added to the collar, do not put the trim on the collar at this time. Simply allow an excess for this trim. Baste the collar to the jacket. Try on the jacket to make sure that the collar is fitting properly and that it's at the proper position on your neck.

Note: If the neck of your jacket is quite a bit larger than your collar, several inches in fact, measure around your neck to the exact point you want your jacket collar to fit. You will need to crochet an edge on the jacket neck, holding the edge in to the desired number of inches. Then apply the collar as explained. But for now, you are only basting the collar in place to have a fitting. If you are satisfied with the fit of the jacket, remove your bastings and proceed to assemble your garment according to the instructions given on page 66.

Put the trim on the collar and on the front edges. Do not simply start in crocheting on these edges. This work must be sectioned off and worked ever so meticulously. Review pages 170–172 for crocheting edges. Now sew the collar to the jacket and add the ribbon facing to the front edges. This information will be found under "Finishing Details" on pages 181 and 184.

JACKETS WITH RAGLAN SLEEVES

If the pattern you have selected is a raglan, you must be on the specified row gauge, or your raglan will be too short or too long. After you have decided upon the size that is correct for your *crochet measurements*, diagram the jacket back as given in the pattern, placing the decreases for the raglan where the pattern states.

Using the following instructions as an example, draw this diagram:

> Back—Ch 99. Work in pat on 48 pats for 15″, end on pat row 3. Piece should measure 19″ wide. *Shape Raglan Armholes*: Bind off 1 pat each side of next row. Dec 1 pat each side every other row 17 times—12 pats left at neck edge. End off.

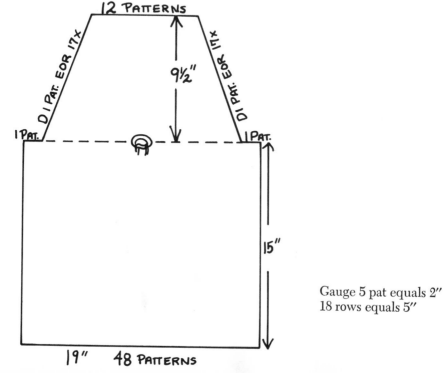

Gauge 5 pat equals 2″
18 rows equals 5″

In the above example the stitch gauge is five patterns equals two inches and the row gauge is eighteen rows equals five inches. If your crocheting is on gauge, your raglan will measure approximately nine and one-half inches straight up from the row of the first bind-off for the armhole shaping. Be sure to tie in a marker in the middle of the row of the first bind-off so that you can measure correctly. See page 47.) This was figured mathematically by adding up all of the rows from the point of the first bind-off for the entire raglan shaping. If you were to decrease every other row seventeen times, it would take you thirty-four rows to work the raglan. Thirty-four divided by the row gauge of eighteen rows equals five inches is approximately nine and one-half inches. If you are obtaining another row gauge, your raglan length will not be the needed nine and one-half inches. After you have worked part way on the jacket, stop and block the piece to the needed width measurement. Then bring the piece up and down as far as possible, still maintaining the width measurement. This will insure that the lengthwise stretch has been accounted for. When the piece is dry, measure out nine and one-half inches of the blocked work and count the number of rows. Place on your diagram the number of rows needed to make up the nine and one-half inch raglan depth. If you need more than thirty-four rows (the amount the pattern calls for), you must space your decreases farther apart so that you will finish with enough rows to make the nine and one-half inch measurement. For example, if you should need four extra rows, show on your diagram that at one inch from the marker you will skip a decrease row; at two inches, skip a decrease row; at three inches, skip; at four inches, skip. From that point on, you will work decreases as specified in your pattern.

Note: The procedure of skipping a decrease row will require that you decrease on a wrong-side row several times, but after

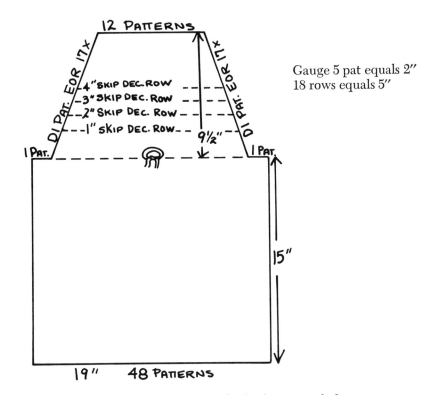

Gauge 5 pat equals 2″
18 rows equals 5″

all of the skip decrease rows have been worked, the rest of the decreases will then be made on right-side rows.

Since all raglans must be the same (because they will be seamed together), whatever you did for the back in the way of skip rows must also be done for the fronts and the sleeves. If you needed skip rows on the back of the jacket, you will also need skip rows on the fronts and the sleeves. Place the skip rows every one inch four times on the fronts and on the sleeves. When it is time to shape the front neck, draw the front neck shaping on a diagram of the front of the jacket.

DOUBLE-BREASTED JACKETS

If the jacket pattern you are going to use is double-breasted, you must know how much overlap the right front has over the left front in order to choose the correct size from which to work. Add up the back stitches and the front stitches required in the pattern just before the underarm shaping. Now read through the directions for the *right front* to find the position of the buttonholes.

> *Example*: Work same as left front to 6″ from beg, ending at front edge. *Next row*—Work 4 sts, ch 3 sts, sk 3 sts, work 12 sts, ch 3 sts, sk 3 sts, work to end. On the next row work 3 sts over the 3 ch sts on each buttonhole—2 buttonholes made.

You must find the center of the overlap. In order to do this, notice that twelve stitches were skipped before the last buttonhole was made. Therefore, the center will be placed in the center of the twelve stitches. Each half of the overlap will involve thirteen stitches.

> 6 half of the twelve center stitches
> 3 the buttonhole stitches
> 4 the stitches worked before start of buttonhole
> ――
> 13

If each half of the overlap is thirteen stitches, the whole overlap will be twenty-six stitches. Add up all of the stitches, back and fronts. Deducting one overlap and then dividing by your stitch gauge will give you your jacket size. Using the above example again, the stitch gauge is nine stitches equals two inches.

> 88 stitches—back
> 57 stitches—front
> 57 stitches—front
> ――
> 202 stitches
>
> −26 deduct one overlap
> ――
> 176 stitches

$$\begin{array}{r} 39.0 \quad \text{the size} \\ \text{stitch gauge } 4.5\overline{)176.0} \\ \underline{135} \\ 410 \\ \underline{405} \\ 5 \end{array}$$

6 Skirts

Custom-Made Skirts
Measurements for skirts
Drafting a pattern for a straight skirt
Working the straight skirt
Finishing skirts
A-line or flared skirts
Skirts with a zipper closing

6 Skirts

CUSTOM-MADE SKIRTS

You can make a skirt to match any jacket or shell by drafting your own skirt pattern from your own personal measurements. Do not try to adjust a skirt pattern from a pattern book. The skirt will not fit your figure as well as a skirt that has been planned for your exact measurements. The measurements at your hips and waist and the distance from your hips to your waist or the total length are not likely to conform exactly to the measurements the pattern maker used when writing the directions for the pattern book.

Measurements for Skirts

Have a second party take your actual body measurements and have them taken in your slip, since you plan to wear the skirt directly over a slip. Tie a ribbon or a tape at your exact waistline. Always stand with your feet together whenever you are having your hips measured (this can make a difference in your actual measurements of up to two inches). Stand in front of a full-length mirror. Your waist should be measured where the ribbon shows your exact waistline to be. Next, the hip measurement should be taken through the fullest part of your hips. Then the tape measure should be brought up above your hips very slowly to see how far it may be raised before your body tapers in toward the waist. The distance from the hips to the waist (from the point where your

138

body starts to taper) should then be measured. If your abdomen is larger than your hips, have your abdomen measurement taken and also the distance down from the waist to the abdomen. In such a case, the abdomen measurement will take the place of the hip measurement so that the finished skirt will not cup in under the "tummy." Lastly, the distance from your waist to the length *you* want the finished skirt should be measured. You may use fractions here, but when drawing up your pattern for crocheting, round off all fractions for width-wise measurments to the nearest inch. Show all of these measurements on a little drawing. Label the drawing "actual body measurements." On a second sheet of paper, draw your crochet measurements. These measurements differ from your actual body measurements at the waist and hips by adding two inches more. This amount of allowance is needed in order to insure a perfect fit. The length from the waist to the hips and the overall length of the skirt are the same in both sets of measurements. See Drawing 1, Actual Body Measurements, and Drawing 2, Crochet Measurements.

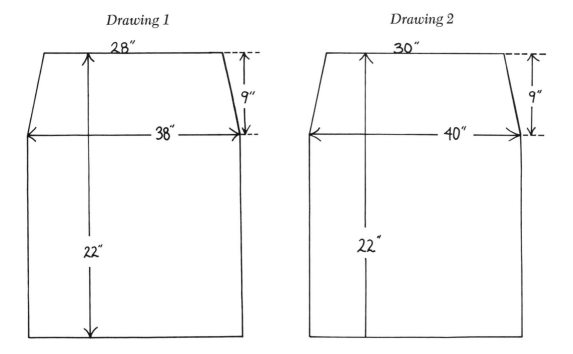

Drawing 1   *Drawing 2*

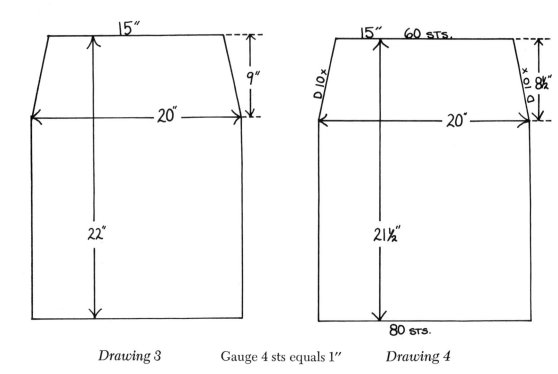

Drawing 3   Gauge 4 sts equals 1″   *Drawing 4*

Drafting a Pattern for a Straight Skirt

Since this skirt will be made in two pieces, the crochet measurements must now be divided into two. The front and back of a crochet skirt should always have the same dimensions. Show half of skirt measurements. See Drawing 3. All of the decreases will be placed at the side edges of the skirt. Notice that on Drawing 4, which is the start of pattern, the total length of the skirt has been shortened by one-half inch—that half inch being subtracted from the top part of the skirt. Later, when the skirt pieces are finished, blocked, and sewed together, a half-inch band will be crocheted on top of the skirt at the waistline. This will account for the missing one-half inch.

In Drawing 4, reading from the bottom of the drawing, the

inch measurement of twenty inches was multiplied by the stitch gauge of four stitches equals one inch. Therefore, eighty stitches were used to start the bottom edge of the skirt. Next, the waist measurement of fifteen inches was multiplied by the gauge, which equals sixty stitches. Sixty, the number of stitches needed for the waist, is subtracted from eighty, the number of stitches needed for the bottom, which equals twenty stitches. By this subtraction you will notice that ten stitches must be decreased on each side of the skirt above the hip line markers, and these decreases must be completed in eight and one-half inches.

> 80 stitches at bottom of skirt
> —60 stitches needed for waist—therefore,
> _____
> 20 stitches must be decreased
> (10 decreases on each side of skirt)

Note: It is best to place the decreases by taking all of your measurements from the bottom of the skirt. Therefore, the first decrease will come when the skirt measures fourteen inches; the second decrease will come when the skirt measures fifteen inches, and so forth.

Study Drawing 5 (completed pattern from which you will work), and notice that markers were placed at the hip line, but no decreases were taken until above the hips. They were placed one inch apart five times; then they were placed every half inch— the last one at eight inches.

When you are drafting your *own* skirt pattern, make the outline drawing of your skirt and place the hip line markers at the proper place. Then draw lines above the hip line markers—as many lines as the number of decreases you need. Figure how you will place these decreases as to inches or half inches so that you will get them all in and accounted for by the time you reach the top of the skirt. Do not take any decreases right at the hip line,

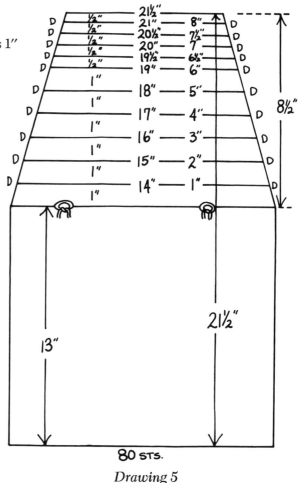

Gauge 4 sts equals 1″

Drawing 5

as this is where you need the full allowance. Space your decreases farther apart when you first start decreasing. If you need to space them closer together to get them in and accounted for by the time you reach the waistline, do so. The body (from the hips up to the waist) tapers gradually to begin with; then toward the waist, the body tapers sharply.

If you are working in a shell pattern or in a pattern containing *long* stitches, your measurements taken from the bottom of the skirt will tell you when to take the decreases, but since these stitches are *long*, your measurements will be longer *after* you have finished the row with the decreases on each side. This, the fact that the stitch is longer, is the reason why the last decrease (in Drawing 5) was not taken at eight and one-half inches. If you are working with shorter stitches, such as single crochet stitches, you may need to add a row or two at the very top of the skirt to make up the needed fraction of an inch.

Working the Straight Skirt

When you are actually working your skirt from the pattern you have drafted, it is most important to stop and block all along the way, as your skirt may drop in length and you should know this. If you are, for example, to take decreases every inch, count out how many rows that will be–directly on the portion of blocked skirt–then place them accordingly as to rows. Be sure to circle your decreases as you do them, and count the number of stitches *after* each decrease row so that you can keep your place on your skirt pattern.

Finishing Skirts

Wash and block the skirt pieces to your crochet measurements (Drawing 2). You should block the pieces one-half inch shorter than your total length so that when the crochet band has been worked, the skirt will be the exact length measurement on *your* Drawing 2.

Wash your skirt pieces according to the washing directions given on page 60. Then, block the first piece with the right side up on the padded surface. Bring the skirt piece out to meet the hip line measurements. Make the bottom edge of the skirt straight and to the same measurements as the hips. With the palms of your hands, gently smooth the piece down until you reach the length measurement from the bottom to the hip line. Now bring the upper part of the skirt out and up to the measurements needed. (Since you have been blocking the piece as you proceeded with your crochet work, you know how much the skirt piece will stretch in length during blocking). Therefore, there should not be any more stretch in the piece than you accounted for. Take a check on the overall length measurement at this time. Work with the bottom edge and the top edge to make them even and straight. Work with the side edges in the same manner. When you come to the place where the tapering begins (above the hip markers), round off the edges so that there will not be a sharp angle at the beginning of the tapering. After you are satisfied with the looks of the first skirt piece, lay out the second piece of the skirt on top of the first piece, with right sides facing each other. Smooth out the skirt as best you can with the wrong side facing you. Make sure that the bottom and top edges are straight. If you wish, you may place drinking glasses, fruit jars, or pop bottles along all edges to insure that the skirt pieces will not draw up during drying. Leave the two skirt pieces together during the entire drying process.

Note: It is advisable to change the towels during the drying process. This will entail some measuring again, but the pieces will dry more quickly.

After the skirt pieces are completely dry, baste the side edges together and try on the skirt for a fitting before seaming the pieces together. If you are satisfied that the skirt fits properly, carefully sew the pieces together according to instructions given in "Assembling" on page 66. Steam the seams with caution so that they are not stretched because stretching will cause the skirt to droop on the sides.

You are now ready to work three or four rows of crochet over tube elastic for the waistband. You must first shrink the tube elastic. Then, when it has dried, cut three or four pieces to fit your waist plus one inch. Cut all pieces the same length. Take one strand of elastic at a time and lap the ends of the elastic over one another. With sewing thread, carefully sew the piece into a circle. Try on the circle of elastic to see if it fits your waist properly. If so, sew all the other pieces of elastic into circles in the same manner. Then section off the circles into halves and fourths, using a pencil to mark the quarters. Section the top of the skirt into fourths. Use the side seams as the halves; then find the center of each piece. Insert pins into the fourths of the skirt. With safety pins, pin the elastic to the top of the skirt, matching markings at the fourths. Join your yarn and work a row of single crochet stitches—one in each stitch at the top of the skirt—working over the elastic. (See drawing.) Join and finish off the round. Now, work over the next circle of tube elastic as before, and continue for two or three more rounds (to measure approximately one-half inch), joining and fastening off after each round. *Do not* steam this band.

Note: Avoid making the elastic too tight, or you will find the skirt uncomfortable.

Finish the bottom edge of the skirt with a row of single crochet stitches (or whatever edging is required), working in each stitch. Steam lightly on the wrong side.

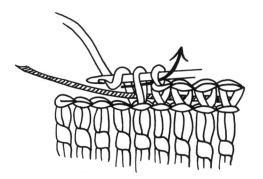

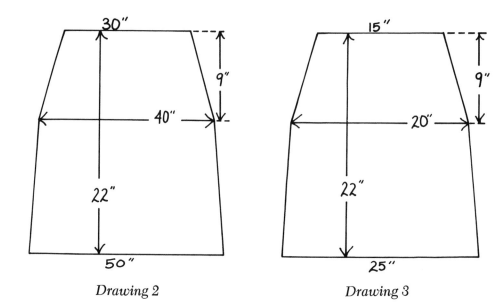

Drawing 2   Drawing 3

A-Line or Flared Skirts

You may wish to make a different type of skirt other than the straight skirt. If you want to make an A-line skirt or a slightly flared skirt, this can easily be done by adjusting the diagrams of your straight skirt. Label all of your new drawings "A-line." By drawing separate diagrams, you will not become confused if you later wish to use the first set of diagrams for other straight skirts.

Stand in front of a full-length mirror and have someone hold the tape measure around your body at the place where the bottom edge of the skirt will be. The tape measure must be held in such a way as to indicate the width you desire your finished skirt to be. If you want a slight A-line skirt, have the tape held out approximately ten inches more than the needed measurement for your hips. Working from your Drawing 2, and making a new A-line Drawing 2, show the bottom edge measurement. See Drawing 2, A-line crochet measurements, adjusted to the wider bottom edge, and Drawing 3, A-line showing half of the skirt measurements. Notice Drawing 4, A-line showing the actual pattern from which you will work. All of the decreases will be placed on the side edges of the skirt. Notice that on A-line Drawing 4, the total length of the skirt has been shortened by one-half inch; that half inch was subtracted from the top part of the skirt, which was also done for the straight skirt pattern, Drawing 4, shown on page 140.

Study Drawing 4, A-line. This skirt pattern is exactly like Drawing 4 for the upper part of the straight skirt (from the hips to the waist); however, the new bottom edge measurement was converted into stitches by multiplying twenty-five inches by the stitch gauge (four stitches equals one inch), or one hundred

Drawing 4 Gauge 4 sts equals 1″

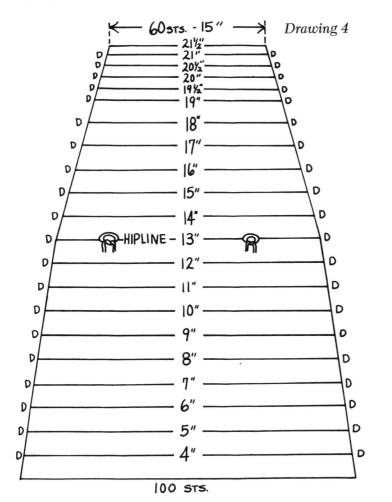

stitches. Next, subtract eighty stitches (number of stitches needed above the hip line markers) from one hundred stitches (number of stitches at bottom of skirt); this equals twenty stitches.

> 100 stitches at bottom of skirt
> —80 stitches needed above hip line markers—therefore,
> 20 stitches must be decreased
> (10 decreases on each side of the skirt)

By this subtraction, you will notice that ten stitches must be decreased on each side of the skirt below the hip line markers. These decreases must be fairly evenly spaced to give the skirt edges a gradual tapering line.

Note: Since it is best to place the decreases by taking all of the measurements from the bottom of the skirt, the first decrease will come when the skirt measures four inches; the second, when the skirt measures five inches, and so forth.

When you are drafting your own skirt pattern for Drawing 4, the A-line skirt, make the outline drawing of your skirt and place the hip line markers at the proper place. Copy the decreases on the upper part of the skirt your Drawing 4, your straight skirt. Then draw lines below the hip line markers—as many lines as you need to take decreases, including one decrease that you take *at* the hip line marker. If you cannot evenly space your decreases, space out your decreases farther apart when you first start decreasing and make them closer together near the end of the decreasing.

Note: When you are actually working your skirt from the pattern you have drafted, you must stop and block the first skirt piece all along the way, as you were advised to do with *any* crochet garment. Your skirt may drop in length and you should know if this has happened. Circle the decreases on your diagram as you do them; then, count the number of stitches *after* each decrease row. Cautious work here can eliminate much ripping and reworking later.

Finish your skirt according to the finishing details given on page 143.

Skirts with a Zipper Closing

If you are working in a sturdy stitch, such as a single crochet stitch, a half double crochet stitch, or a double crochet stitch, you may wish to use a zipper closing and a crocheted waistband on your skirt. However, it is not advisable to use a zipper closing if your skirt was worked in a lacy pattern stitch because the zipper tape will show through the holes in the pattern on the outside of the garment. For open, lacy pattern stitches, see the finishing details for skirts using crochet over tube elastic, page 144.

The two-piece skirt will need to be seamed on each side (see directions for "Assembling," page 66). The left side must be left unseamed for the zipper from a point seven inches from the top of the skirt. Next, steam out the side seams. Place one row of single crochet stitches around the zipper opening on the left side. Be sure to follow the directions given on page 173 for working this edge. Measure the opening and make sure that the length is the exact length of the zipper teeth (or chain). The zipper will not be sewed in at this time. Since you will be starting your waistband using the same strand of yarn, do not fasten off the yarn at the end of the zipper opening.

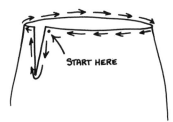

With pins, divide the waist of the skirt into eight equal sections, placing pins at the end of each section. Begin by dividing the skirt into fourths. You will notice that the halfway pin will come at the opposite seam (the right side seam). Other pins will be placed at the center front and at the center back of the skirt. Now divide each quarter space into half. This gives you eight equal sections.

Measure your waist and draw a little diagram showing all eight of the sections and how many inches each section should be when completed. See the drawing, which is for a waist of twenty-eight inches.

Take up the yarn which is waiting at the top of the skirt (left front side) and place two stitches at the very corner to allow for a turn. Work along the first section, holding the work in to the desired inch measurement. In the example, the first section should measure three and one-half inches. If the first section meets the required inch measurement, count the number of stitches you used in that section. Work across the second, the third, and the fourth sections in the same manner, using the number of stitches you used in the first section. You should now be at the right side seam. Stop here and measure the entire distance. It should measure one-half of your waist measurement. If the measurement is not correct, you must rework the first half of the skirt, making the necessary adjustment. When you have finished one row of single crochet, measure the skirt waist. If the measurement is correct, single crochet three more rows, checking measurements after each row. At the end of the last row, make a chain loop of approximately four chain stitches and join the loop to the bottom of the crochet band, and fasten off the yarn. Work in the end. Next, steam the crochet edge around the zipper closing and the crochet band. Make sure that you do not stretch the band while steaming. Sew in the zipper according to the directions given on page 187.

The skirt band is now ready to be reinforced with grosgrain ribbon. Buy a length of three-quarter inch grosgrain ribbon of matching color several inches longer than your waist measurement. Preshrink the ribbon and press it. Cut the piece of ribbon the length of your waist measurement plus one-half inch, to allow for turning under the edges. The ribbon will be pinned to the wrong side of the waistband approximately one-fourth inch below the top of the band. Cover the ends of the zipper tape with the grosgrain ribbon. Divide the ribbon in half with a straight pin and pin the halfway marking to the center of the right side seam. Distribute any fullness evenly so that the band looks smooth from the outside. Using matching sewing thread, and with very small stitches, sew the ribbon to the top edge of the band (one-fourth inch below where you have pinned it).

Note: By pinning and sewing the ribbon slightly below the top edge, you insure that the ribbon will not show from the right side.

When working the bottom edge of the grosgrain ribbon band, you will notice that the ribbon will extend beyond the crocheted

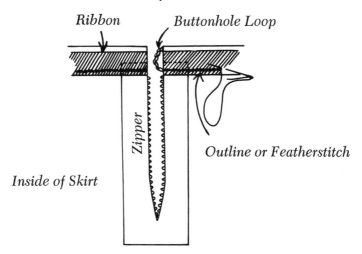

Ribbon   *Buttonhole Loop*

Zipper

Outline or Featherstitch

Inside of Skirt

waistband by approximately one-fourth inch, and if you were to sew this edge down as you did the top edge, you would be sewing into the skirt itself and not in the crocheted band. With sewing thread, make an even row of outline stitches (or another pretty embroidery stitch, such as a featherstitch) approximately one-fourth inch from the bottom edge of the ribbon. See the drawing for working the outline stitch or the featherstitch. This will hold the ribbon firmly at the bottom of the band, and the stitching will add a pretty, hand-finished look. Steam the band with the wet washcloth method; then sew a flat button in place opposite the crocheted loop.

Featherstitch   *Outline Stitch*

Outside View of Skirt

7 Dresses

General

Measurements to Take for Dresses

Adapting a Dress Pattern to Fit Your Figure
Diagrams

Crocheting the Dress
Shaping the front neckline

Assembling and Finishing
Problem seams
Extra finishing details

7 Dresses

GENERAL

Do not attempt to crochet a dress for your first crochet garment. The fitting and blocking of a dress requires considerable background. You must work up to it by making simple single pieces, such as shells and skirts.

You will not be able to follow a pattern in a pattern book without making adjustments to fit your figure. Exeryone has different measurements at the hips, waist, bust, and shoulders and the distance from the hips to the waist, the length of the skirt, and the length of the bodice. Do not make your dress without first making sure that the dress will fit you when you have finished your crocheting. You will not want to make any drastic alterations after the dress is finished, so the best thing is to custommake the dress to your *own* body measurements.

Most patterns for dresses are made in two pieces—a front and a back. Decreases and increases are used on the side edges to shape the pieces for the waist, bust, and shoulders. However, some patterns requiring a lacy all-over pattern stitch will have you change the size of the hook to be used in order to make the pieces smaller, instead of taking decreases which would disturb the symmetry of the pattern stitch. Your dress, with this change of hooks, will get the necessary shaping. Read and understand this type of pattern thoroughly. You will need to work separate stitch gauges for each of the hook sizes required so that you will know exactly how much smaller you are making the dress at each of the key places on your basic dress measurement chart.

MEASUREMENTS TO TAKE FOR DRESSES

Take your actual measurements as you did when you were planning your jacket and skirt patterns (review pages 120 and 138). You may use fractions when taking the actual dress measurements, but when you draw your pattern for crocheting, round off all fractions for width measurements (except shoulders) to the nearest inch. Wear a good foundation garment, and since you will be wearing the dress over a slip, have the measurements taken in your slip. Stand in front of a full-length mirror. Stand with your feet together whenever you are having your hips measured. Tie a ribbon or a tape around your waist, and then adjust it to your exact waistline. Have someone take all of the measurements for you. Make a drawing, showing all of your measurements: your bust (through the fullest part of the bust), your shoulders (through your back from shoulder bone to shoulder bone), your waist, and your hips (through the fullest part of your hips). Have these lengths measured: the length from the nape of your neck to your exact waist, the length from your waist to your hips, the total length of the skirt from your waist to the bottom edge of the dress. Next, have the distance measured from the nape of your neck to the bottom edge of the dress. Compare that figure with the length of the bodice from the back of the neck plus the skirt length. If there is any discrepancy, have the measurements taken over again and make the necessary correction. See Drawing 1 for an example of actual measurements that are required for making

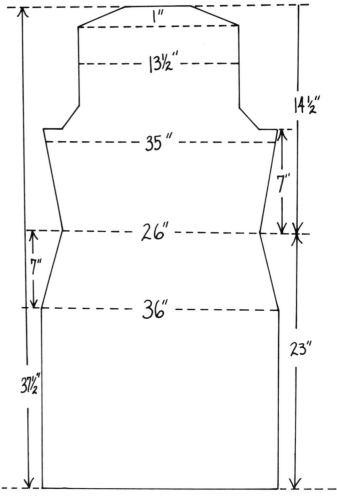

Drawing 1

a dress. Notice that approximately one inch is allowed from the nape of the neck to the place where the shoulder shaping *starts*. This is always shown on the measurement drawings.

Carefully study Drawing 2, crochet measurements. The necessary allowances have been taken (more than your actual body measurements) to insure a perfect fit. These allowances are: two inches more at the bust, the waist, and the hips, and *no* allowance

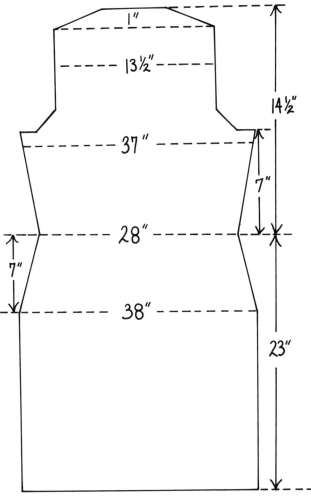

Drawing 2

at all for the shoulders. Dresses require a closer fit than jackets and they are usually made of a lighter weight yarn. For these reasons, only two inches more at the bust is allowed as compared with the three to four inches allowed for jackets.

Note: If you do not allow at least two inches at the waist, you will not be able to get the dress on over your head, unless you plan a side opening with a placket zipper. This is not necessary

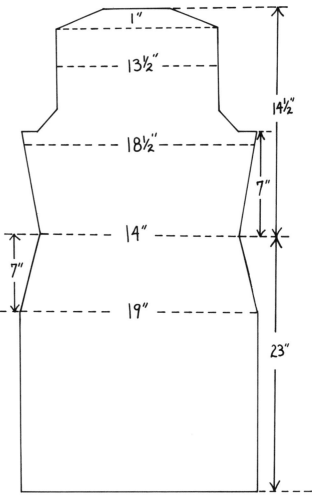

Drawing 3

in most crocheted dresses, and many people feel that a zipper here detracts from the looks of the dress. The lines of many dresses do not fit into the waist at all, or they may fit just slightly. Belts or ties can then be placed at the waist, or below the waist, or just above the hipbones. If your dress does have a definite tight waist, an elastic band should be worked into the waist after the dress is completed. See page 167 for working this band into the finished dress.

See Drawing 3, half of crochet measurements. Divide all of your measurements in half and show them on *your* Drawing 3, half of crochet measurements. The front and back of crocheted dresses (or skirts) should always be the same dimensions.

ADAPTING A DRESS PATTERN TO FIT YOUR FIGURE

Before you can adapt a dress pattern to your own measurements, you must first diagram the pattern as it is given in the pattern book. When choosing the size from which you will work, take the size closest to your needed bust measurement. (This is not your actual bust measurement; it is your bust measurement plus the two-inch allowance.)

Read carefully through the instructions until you come upon the number of stitches or patterns called for at the bustline. Add up the stitches on the back and the front at the bustline; then divide by the stitch gauge in order to get the size in inches at the bust. The number of stitches at the bust will be the number the pattern carries just before the shaping of the underarm.)

Diagrams

Draw the diagram of the back of the dress according to the pattern then change stitches into inches (by dividing by your stitch gauge) at all key places on the diagram. The key places are: the bottom edge, the hips, the waist, the bust, the shoulders, the neck, and any other important place where changes take place. See

Drawing 4, a crocheted dress pattern. The pattern for the dress in Drawing 4 reads as follows:

> *Gauge*: 5 ch-1 spaces equals 2″; 9 rows equals 2″.
>
> *Back*: Ch 106 sts.
>
> *Row 1*: Work 1 sc in 2nd ch from hook and in each ch across row. 105 sc; ch 2, turn.
>
> *Row 2*: 1 sc in first sc, * ch 1, skip 1, 1 sc in next sc, repeat from * across, ending 1 sc in last sc, ch 2, turn.
>
> *Row 3*: 1 sc in first ch-1 space, * ch 1, 1 sc in next space, repeat from * across ending 1 sc in turning ch, ch 2 turn.
>
> Repeat Row 3 for pat working on 53 ch-1 spaces for 11″ from start. Dec 1 space each side on next row as follows:
>
> Skip 1st space, 1 sc in next space, ch 1, work in pat across, skipping next to last space, ending 1 sc in turning ch, ch 2, turn.
>
> Keeping pat as established, dec 1 space each side every 3″ 4 times more. Work on 43 spaces to 24″ or desired length to waistline. Mark for waist. Work in pat for 3″ above waist. Inc 1 space each side of next row as follows:
>
> 1 sc in first sc, * ch 1, 1 sc in next space, repeat from * ending ch 1, 1 sc in turning ch (2 ch-1 spaces increased).
>
> Keeping pat as established, inc 1 space each side when 6″ above waist marker.
>
> Work even on 47 pat to 7½″ above marker.
>
> *Shape armholes*: Sl st across first 3 spaces, ch 2, work in pat across, ending 1 sc in 4th space from end of row, ch 2, turn. Dec 1 space each side every row 2 times. Work on the 37 spaces for 6¾″ straight above underarm, ending at armhole edge. Omit the ch 2 at end of last row.

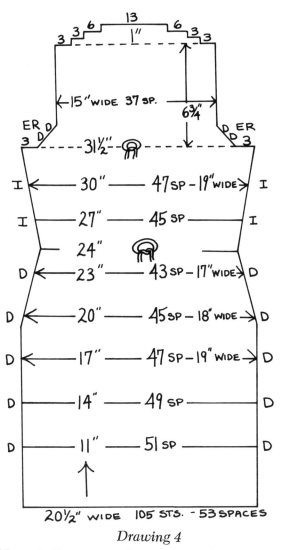

Gauge 5 ch
1 sps equals 2″
9 rows equals 2″

Drawing 4

Shoulders: * Sl st across 3 spaces, work in pat to last 3 spaces, work 1 row in pat, omitting the ch 2 turn, repeat from * once more. Sl st across 6 spaces, work across 13 spaces, leaving 6 spaces unworked on other shoulder. Fasten off.

The instructions for the front and the sleeves of the dress will not be given here. Instructions for the back appear in Drawing 4, Diagram of Dress Back, so that you may see just how the back of the dress would have to be worked.

The next step in working over the original diagram (Drawing 4) is to change stitches (or patterns) into inches at all of the key points on the diagram. This has been done on the sample diagram. The length measurements have also been inserted.

Study Drawing 5, which shows how the back pattern was adjusted to the measurements of Drawing 3, half of crochet measurements.

Note: In order to draw this diagram step by step, the shape of the dress back was drawn first, then the inch measurements needed from Drawing 3, half of crochet measurements, were shown, then finally, the inches were changed into patterns (or stitches) at the places where the pattern needed adjustment to conform to the exact measurements of Drawing 3.

CROCHETING THE DRESS

You will not want to guess about any phase of crocheting your dress. For this reason, you must block your stitch gauge carefully. Then you must block several times during the process of crocheting the dress. You have been urged to do this throughout this book whenever you make any garment. Too much time is involved in crocheting and you will certainly not want to spend additional time shortening parts of the dress or ripping and reworking parts. The dress can be crocheted right the first time if you block as you proceed with your work. Lengths in crochet garments present a serious problem. Because crochet work has a tendency to stretch in length, the best procedure to follow is to work approximately eight or ten inches on the back skirt piece; then stop and block that much. Bring the piece out to your

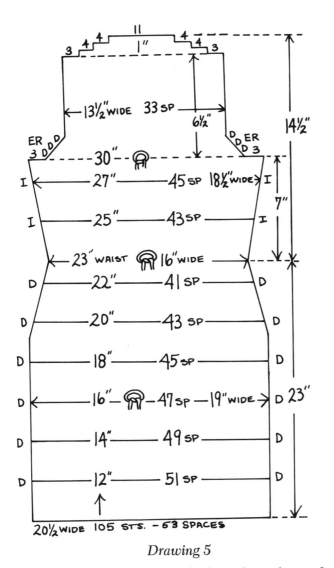

Gauge 5 ch
1 sps equals 2″
9 rows equals 2″

Drawing 5

needed width measurement, then with the palms of your hands, smooth up and down as far as you can stretch it in length—still maintaining the width measurement. In this way, you will be getting all of the lengthwise stretch out of your work. Let the piece dry completely. Now take the length measurement again, and if your work "grew" in length, you now have a fair idea of how much the entire finished garment will stretch. However, do not assume that you need not block again at the waist and bust and after the back is completely finished. The longer the piece becomes, the more gravity works on it and the more stretch in length you may have.

Note: If you notice that the partial dress is drawing in width-wise as it is drying, re-wet it and weight down the edges with something heavy, such as drinking glasses, fruit jars or pop bottles. If the skirt part of the dress will not block out to the needed width measurement without much stretching, you have not maintained the stitch gauge. In such a case, you would be wise to start again—adjusting your hook size.

After the first blocking at approximately eight to ten inches, count rows or patterns, and if you are to work, for example, six inches more before you reach the hip line, measure out six inches on the blocked portion of your dress. Count *that* number of rows or patterns and work *that* number of rows or patterns to the hip line. Continue on with the skirt part of your dress, taking decreases at the side edges as specified on your diagram, and work until you come to the waist. Block again at this point. Block again at the underarm point to your needed width, smoothing the pieces with the palms of your hands as before to remove all lengthwise stretch. If you must remove rows because the work "grew," be sure to do so before proceeding further. Block once more after you have finished the entire dress back.

You are now ready to start the front of your dress. You need not block this piece at all because you will be counting rows (or patterns), and taking your decreases and increases on the same numbered row as for the back.

Shaping the Front Neckline

You may run into difficulty when you are shaping the front neck edge, especially if you are working in a lacy pattern stitch. Your instructions may tell you step by step exactly how to work the left front neck edge. If this is the case, the pattern may read, for example, "Finish right neck edge, reversing the shaping." This can present quite a problem, especially if your pattern stitch is staggered. The only way you can make the two front neck edges look the same is to use the comparison method at this point on each and every row of the front neck edges. Mark with a safety pin the row you are to copy on the completed left front neck edge. Count patterns across to the armhole edge, and then try to duplicate the same thing on the right neck edge, using the same number of patterns.

ASSEMBLING AND FINISHING

Read through the instructions for finishing details that are given in your pattern. Many times these directions are very vague and do not give the instructions in the proper sequence.

After the dress pieces are completed and have been washed and blocked, carefully baste them together at the shoulders. Next, baste in the sleeves and then baste the sides together, matching rows or patterns. Now try on the dress for a fitting before you assemble it.

Follow the sequence in putting your dress together as you were instructed to do for your first project. Carefully review pages 66–70 for proper sequence and assembling methods. Steam each seam before making any cross seams.

Problem Seams

If your dress is in a lacy open pattern stitch, you may have long sections of chain stitches on the side edges of your garment. If such is the case, you will need to do a little experimenting as to where to place the stitches, or you may find that you have large gaping holes where these long chains appear. If you were to sew them right on the very edge, *two* chains would show after the seam is completed. Since you want only *one* chain to show, you must conceal half of each chain on the inside of the seam on each piece. Working from the right side, take a very small stitch through the center of the chain on one piece; then take a small stitch through the center of the matching chain on the other piece. With the thumbnail, push both edges to the wrong side to form a *very small flat seam.* Continue to take stitch for stitch until you reach firmer crochet work. (See drawing.)

Occasionally you may have to resort to using a backstitch for seams on certain types of stitches to be joined. (Backstitched seams are worked from the wrong side.) Such an instance would be if you have to join "joggy" edges together, the result of decreases which could not be made without leaving jogs. Use very small backstitches, keeping the seam line straight. (See drawing of backstitch.)

You would also have to use a backstitch if there were any large holes on the edges because of decreases in certain pattern stitches. Examine the edges carefully before starting to seam, and if necessary, try out several of the methods explained and then decide which method looks best for your particular problem seams.

Extra Finishing Details

After the seaming has been completed to your satisfaction, add all trim—collar, crochet edges, pockets, etc. Consult the pattern finishing details for instructions and review pages 170–189 for correct methods.

If your dress is to be worn with a belt, you may want to put in a very lightweight elastic on the inside of the dress exactly at the waist line. This elastic will be inconspicious from the outside. Try on the dress and mark the waist. Turn the dress inside out and run a basting line on the marked waistline to help you crochet this edge straight. Crochet one row of * slip stitch into a stitch directly on the line marked for the waist, then chain two or three stitches, then skip approximately one-half inch at the marked waistline, and repeat from * around the waist. Fasten off and work in the end of yarn. Cut a length of one-eighth inch elastic (be sure to preshrink it) slightly longer than your waist measurement. Weave the elastic in and out through the crochet edge you have just formed. Next, try on the dress and adjust the elastic for a comfortable fit. Sew the elastic securely. This elastic worked into the waistline will help to keep the dress from sagging, as it might if the entire weight of the dress were hanging from the shoulders.

8 Other Finishing Details

Adding Trim or Edging
   Crochet edges
   Borders
      Buttonholes
   Crocheting around the entire jacket
      Using contrasting color for edges or borders

Sewing on Collars

Tacking Pocket Liners

Ribbon Facings

Sewing on Buttons

Zippers

Button Loops

8 Other Finishing Details

ADDING TRIM OR EDGING

Any neck trim, borders, pockets or collars is added after assembling.

Crochet Edges

If any crochet is required around the neck, the armholes, the bottom edge, or the bottom of the sleeves, you must have a plan and follow it. Do not just start in crocheting without any plan or order to your work. You will not have an even look. First, try on the garment and stand in front of a full-length mirror. Take a carfeul look at the neckline. Decide *now* whether the neckline is right or if you want to raise it a little. Measure with your tape around the neckline in the front, starting at the shoulder seam, and measure to the other shoulder seam. Make sure that the tape is not lying flat on your chest or neck, but that it is in a stand-out position at the point where you wish the completed neckline to be. Make a little drawing of the garment showing your measurements for the neckline, armholes, bottom edge, etc. Measure the back neckline in the same manner, measuring from shoulder seam to shoulder seam.

Note: Have someone else do this measuring for you if possible.

Take a good look at the armholes if the garment is sleeveless. With your tape around the armhole in the front of the garment, measure from the shoulder seam to the side seam (half of the armhole), holding the tape as before at the point where you want the

170

armholes to fit. Measure around yourself at the place where the bottom edge of the garment touches your body. This last measurement will insure a snug fit at the bottom edge. Put all of these measurements on the drawing. (See drawing.)

Example: Distance around the front of the neckline—sixteen inches. You must now divide this distance into sections, inserting a straight pin at the end of each section. Fold the neckline into halves and fourths. Join your yarn at the left shoulder. With the right side of your work facing you, work along in single crochet stitches, "trying" for the number of stitches needed in the first section.

Caution! Keep your stitches moderately loose and large, and strive to make them even.

You must be very careful when placing stitches on a curve. It is difficult to find good places in which to put stitches because of the unevenness of the decreases. Do not form a stitch in any place that will leave a large hole. After you have finished edging one section, measure it. It should equal one-fourth of the entire front neckline, or in this example, four inches. This edge should be firm enough

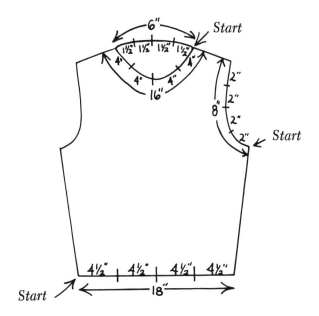

so that you cannot stretch the distance more than four inches. If the first section measured more or less than the needed four inches, count the number of stitches used and work the section over again, taking a few more or a few less stitches, whichever is necessary. Jot down the number of stitches used in the first section. Proceed to the next section and put exactly as many stitches in the second section as you did in the first section. After you have worked the first two sections, take another check on the measurement. The worked edge should now measure eight inches. Since you know how many stitches are needed in each section, continue the other two sections, measuring as you go along. You are now at the other shoulder seam and ready to work across the back. Divide the back part of the neckline into four sections as you did for the front. "Try" for the number of stitches needed in the first section of the back, and when you have decided on the correct number, work that many stitches in each section of the back, making checks on the measurement at the halfway point, at the three-quarter point, and at the end. You should have a very even look to the neckline by using this sectioning method. You now have your neckline established. If another row of crochet is required or a fancy edge, you should work other rows in each stitch.

Work your armhole edging in the same manner as you worked the neck. That is, section off the armhole into four sections for each half of the armhole and proceed as for the neckline. Work the bottom edge, sectioning and keeping track of the stitches in each section.

When all of the crochet work is completed, steam it lightly with the "wet washcloth method." (See page 68.) Work with the edge while it is damp to make it straight. Steam the neck and armhole edges into a curve. Make sure that they are perfect, lest you ruin an otherwise beautiful garment with uneven crochet edgings.

Borders

If crochet borders are required on the front edges of a jacket, the stitches must be placed carefully so that you will have an even look to the finished jacket. You will not want this border to draw in or to be too full. The average crocheter will just begin crocheting on the front border, placing stitches at random up one side and down the other side, with the following results: The two edges might not match—one might be longer than the other. Stitches might be placed too close together on some parts of the edge and too far apart on other parts, giving the edges a "ripply" look. These little finishing details can ruin an otherwise well-made garment. Learn to work these edges correctly!

After the jacket has been washed, blocked, and sewed together, try on the jacket and stand in front of a full-length mirror. Stand so that your side is facing the mirror. You will then be able to see how the front bottom edge of the jacket looks in comparison with the side bottom edge. Notice if the front edges are drooping. Hold the front edges in line with the side bottom edge. Next, measure the length of the front (where your borders will be) with your tape measure, noting the distance from the neck edge to the bottom of the garment, where you are holding it in line with the side. (Have someone else do this measuring for you if possible.) Make a notation of that measurement on a little diagram. See drawing, page 174. Now take the jacket off and lay it out on a flat surface. Measure the front edge while the jacket is lying flat. You will now know if you need to hold the jacket edge in to the needed measurement or to draw it out to meet the needed measurement. In the example, assume that the edge should measure eighteen inches. You must now divide this front into sections, inserting a straight pin at the end of each section. Divide the front into halves, then into fourths. Start with the right side (outside) of your work facing you, on the border that will not have buttonholes (left front for ladies' garments), and "try" for the number of stitches that you will need in the first section. After you have worked the first section, measure the distance with your tape. The distance should measure four and one-half inches, or one-fourth of the total of eighteen inches. If your work measures more or less than the amount you need (one-fourth of the total distance), try the first section over again, either adding stitches or taking some out until you have the *four and one-half inches you need.* Now you know exactly how many stitches you need in each section, so continue up the front, working all sections with the same number of stitches. You must keep measuring at the halfway point—nine inches, at the three-quarter point—thirteen and one-half inches, and, when finished, you will have eighteen inches.

At the end of the first row, if you are to crochet several rows, chain one and turn; then, put a stitch in each stitch of the first foundation row, putting the hook through both top loops.

Caution! When working the second row and all other rows following, make sure that you are working loosely. Measure your work after each row to be certain that you are still maintaining the number of inches you need.

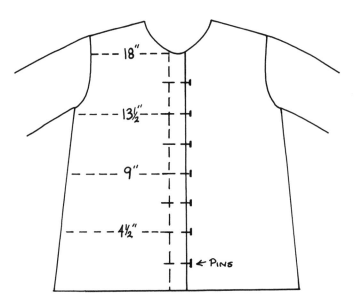

Front of Jacket

BUTTONHOLES

If you are to place buttonholes in the crochet edge, work the side without buttonholes first. When you start to work the side with the buttonholes, section off that side of the front exactly as you did for the other front and place as many stitches in each secion as you did for the first side. When you come to the row in which you are to form the buttonholes, you must locate the spot where the buttonholes are to be formed. Use this method: Mark the position of the first buttonhole and the last buttonhole with a small safety pin directly on the border you have started. Now measure the distance between the two pins. (See page 128 for more information.)

Example: To mark the positions of six buttons, the first button should be one inch above the bottom edge and the last button should be one-half inch from the neck edge. When you have the first and last buttons marked, measure the distance between the pins. If your pattern requires six buttons, you will need five spaces. (You always need one less space than the number of buttons.)

In the above example, assume that the distance between the two pins is seventeen inches. Your button markings will be approximately three inches apart. Seventeen inches divided by five spaces equals (almost) three and one-half inches. You will then place safety pins on the border nearly three and one-half inches apart. Adjust the pins just slightly to make the spaces even.

To crochet the next row and start the buttonholes, place single crochet stitches in each stitch until you come to a stitch or two before the pin; chain two, then skip two single crochet stitches of the previous row; then, single crochet in the next stitch. Try placing the button through the hole. If the hole is too small, chain one or two more stitches, and then skip one or two more single crochet stitches in the previous row. When you are satisfied

Start of Buttonhole

Finished Buttonhole

as to the size of the buttonhole, continue to work all the other buttonholes in the same manner. (See photographs.)

On the following row, work until you come to the buttonhole. Then, if you have skipped two single crochet stitches for the start of the buttonhole, place the same number of single crochet stitches in the chain loop, and then proceed in single crochet stitch to the next hole. Work all of the buttonholes the same. These buttonholes will not need to be hand finished! They will always lie flat.

After you have finished the crochet borders, lay the edges out on your padded ironing board; right sides down, and with the "wet washcloth method," lightly steam each border, measurnig them with the tape measure to make sure that they are the same lengh, and the length that you need.

Crocheting around the Entire Jacket

For crochet edges around the entire jacket, you will use the same procedures you used when you were working the front edge only; that is, you will be sectioning off your entire jacket and keeping track of the number of stitches required for each section.

Try on the jacket. Stand in front of a mirror and look at the bottom edge. Decide whether you are satisfied with the way the jacket fits at the bottom edge. Perhaps you will want to hold in the bottom edge for a closer fit. If so, measure with your tape to the exact number of inches you want the bottom edge to be. Next, measure the center front edge (see page 173) to obtain the number of inches needed there so that the garment will not hang longer in the front than in the back. All of these measurements must be put on your diagram.

Start at the bottom edge, at the side seam of the right front, always working from the right side (outside) of the garment.

Section off the right front bottom edge into four sections. Join the yarn at the seam and count the number of single crochet stitches you can put into the first section. Try placing a stitch in each stitch on the edge (the chain edge where you first started to work the piece). You may find that by going into each stitch the work will be too full. In that case, you may have to skip over one or two stitches to make the work lie flat. If you do have to skip a stitch or two, space out the skips so that they are not right next to each other. Proceed to the next section, making the same number of stitches you decided upon when doing the first section. Then go on to the third and fourth sections. When you come to a corner, you must put three stitches into the same hole in order to make the turn.

You are now at the start of the center front edge. Section off the front edge into eight sections as explained on page 173, keeping track of the number of stitches and measuring at the quarter, half, three-quarter, and finished lengths. You are now ready to work the curved neck edge. Section off the neck edge to the shoulder seam into four sections. You must be careful here be-

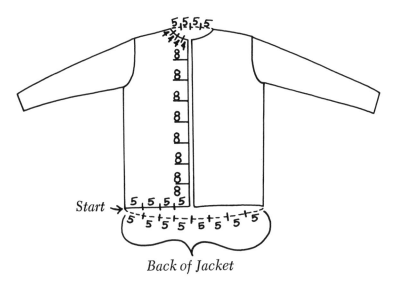

Back of Jacket

cause you are on a curve and it is difficult to find good places to put in your stitches because of the unevenness of the decreases. Do not place stitches where you will leave a large hole. When you have finished the front neck shaping, you will proceed to the back of the neck. Divide this part into four sections and proceed as before. When you are coming around to the other side of the front of the neck shaping, divide it into four sections and put in the same number of stitches that you put in on the other side at the front edge. Proceed down the front, turn the corner (with three stitches as before), sectioning that portion and maintaining the same number of stitches in each section to conform to the first front. Turn another corner (with three stitches as before) and work the bottom edge of the left front exactly like the bottom edge of the first front. Now divide the back into halves, fourths, and eighths. Find out how many stitches go nicely into the first scetion, and then work across all sections alike.

If more than one row of crochet is needed, as you return across the first row, you must place a stitch in each stitch of the previous row, working through both top loops. When turning a corner,

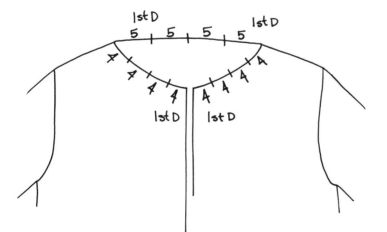

*Neck Shaping Showing Decreases
to Taper in on Second Row*

place three stitches in the center of the corner as explained before. It will be necessary to decrease on the second row (and all other extra rows) of the neck to give it a tapered look. (If you do not decrease, and continue to put a stitch in each stitch as before, you will find that the neck will stand up like a mandarin collar.) If more than two rows are worked, you should not decrease all in one row. Work off three or four decreases in each row. To decrease, you simply pass by a stitch (skip a stitch in the previous row), and then single crochet in the next stitch. The following is another way of decreasing in crochet: draw up a loop in each of the next two stitches, yarn over and pull the hook through both loops on the hook. Of the two methods explained, the first method (skipping a stitch) usually looks best. You can try both and make the decision yourself. Keep track of your decreases on paper (see drawing on page 179), telling you in what section they appeared, so that on the next row you will not decrease in the same section in which you decreased before. Try on the jacket as you are working the rows to determine if more or fewer decreases are needed. Be sure to keep measuring each portion with your tape measure so that you maintain the number of inches needed in each area you sectioned. Many times a person will work the additional rows tighter than she worked the first establishing row. Be on the alert so that this does not happen.

When crocheting around the sleeve edge, divide the sleeve into sections and proceed as for the other parts of the jacket. (See drawing.)

After you have finished the edgings, you must steam them lightly using the "wet washcloth method." Work with the edges and the corners while they are damp, making sure that they are straight and even. Steam the neck edge into a horseshoe curve. (See drawing.)

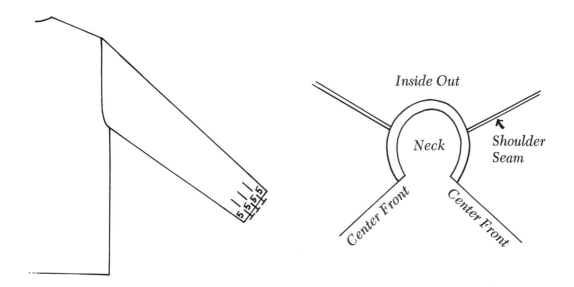

USING CONTRASTING COLOR FOR EDGES OR BORDERS

If you want to put on borders with a contrasting color, work the first establishing row with the main color; then, on the second row, use the contrasting color. If you do not do this, the edges will have an uneven look on the first row, which will spoil the looks of your garment.

SEWING ON COLLARS

Try on the jacket and make sure that the neck edge fits you correctly. If it does, take the measurement of the neck edge and jot it down on your scratch pad. Now divide your total measurement at the jacket neck in half and place a pin in the center (this should be at a point at the center of the back of the neck). Now, divide the halves into halves and place pins at the halfway point. Your jacket or dress neck edge is now divided into fourths. Divide your collar into fourths.

Note: The collar should be washed and blocked to the correct measurement.

Now pin the washed and blocked collar to the finished jacket or dress—matching pins at the fourth and halfway points. Place your beginning pin at the center of the overlap so that when the jacket is buttoned your collar edges will just come together at the front edge and not lap over. Pin the collar so that the outside of the jacket and the wrong side of the collar are facing each other.

Note: You will *not* seam the collar the way it is pinned. If you should do so, your seam would show from the right side. You will be taking out each pin as you come to it as you are sewing, and the seam will fall to the wrong side.

Be sure to measure the distance from the center front where the collar starts to the shoulder seam of the jacket. Then measure the distance from the center front to the shoulder seam on the opposite shoulder seam. The distances should be the same. You must be particular that all sections measure the same number of inches; then the collar will not be lopsided, but will be accurate and even.

Join the yarn, without making a knot, in the manner explained on page 67. You should sew from the right side of the collar and the wrong side of the jacket. Use a *very small* "side-to-side" stitch, taking a stitch on the collar piece just under the edge, with the needle running parallel to the edge of the collar. Then

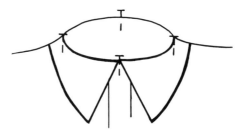

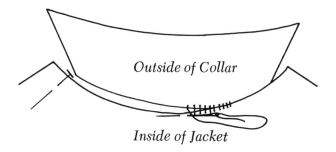

Outside of Collar

Inside of Jacket

take a small stitch on the garment piece, with the needle running parallel to the edge of the neck. Now with the thumbnail, push both edges to the wrong side to form a *very small, flat seam.* You should be using split yarn, if possible, and very short strands of yarn. Check your work as you proceed so that your inch measurements conform to those on your diagram at the shoulder seams and at the halfway (center back) points.

Note: This is the only way a collar can be applied without a heavy seam. If you should put the seam together and sew from the wrong side of the collar, you would not be able to make a seam as small and it would not block flat.

Now steam the seam using the "wet washcloth method," taking many little steps so that the seam is not stretched out of shape. Do not try to open the seam with your fingers, as it is too small a seam and you may stretch the neck edge or collar edge if you should attempt to do so.

TACKING POCKET LINERS

Pin the pocket liners in place, then, with split yarn or sewing thread (if the garment is made of lightweight yarn), carefully sew the liners in place, using the "side-to-side" stitch, and keep the stitches quite close together. Take a little parallel stitch on the edge of the pocket liner; then take another parallel stitch on the garment piece, picking up just a few "hairs" of the yarn so that the stitching will not show on the right side of the garment. Be careful that you do not pull the stitches too tightly. This could cause an impression to show on the right side (outside) of the garment.

RIBBON FACINGS

Occasionally patterns call for a ribbon facing on the front edges of crochet jackets. This is to give more firmness to these edges and to reinforce the buttonholes, and also to make a strong backing for sewing on the buttons.

Buttonholes in crochet garments do not need to be hand finished. Place one row of single crochet stitches on the edges. Do this work according to the instructions given on page 170. The ribbon must be preshrunk and pressed. Now pin the ribbon to the wrong side of one front edge of the preblocked and assembled garment. Try on the garment so that you can see whether the front edge is lying flat and not drawing up or sagging. Readjust the ribbon, if it is necessary. When you are satisfied with the way the jacket hangs, cut the ribbon for the first side, allowing one-fourth inch at the top and bottom edges for turning under. Now cut another length of ribbon exactly the same measurement. Remove the pins from the first facing and fold the ribbon in half to find the center. Find the center of the crochet edge by folding the edge in half in the same manner. Place pins at the top and bottom of the ribbon and at the matching center pins, folding under the one-fourth inch you allowed for this. The ribbon should be pinned to the base of the crochet stitch which you just put on the edges, so that the entire crochet stitch is extending beyond the ribbon. (See drawing.) Place pins all around the ribbon. Use sewing thread in a matching color and start at the outside edge,

Base of
Crochet
Stitch

Ribbon

Wrong
Side

Ribbon Facing

Outside →
Edge

Little "V"

Buttonhole

using very small hemming stitches. Place the stitches very near the edge of the ribbon so that the stitches will not show. Pass the needle through just part of a stitch of yarn so that the sewed stitch will not show from the right side. You must either sew *down* on each side of the ribbon or *up* on each side. You should not sew up one side and then down the other side, because your crochet material is stretchy and, if you do so, the front edge will shift sideways.

When working the inside edge of the ribbon on the buttonhole side, make a small slash in the ribbon to the far end of the button-hole, and then turn under the raw edges in a little V around each buttonhole (see drawing). This is a satisfactory method because one end of the buttonhole is not surrounded by ribbon; thus, the hole may stretch and open up to receive the button.

Ribbon

Crocheted Edge

If you have crochet borders in which the buttonholes are placed, these buttonholes will be vertical. In such a case, you cannot use the slashing and V-ing around the buttonhole as just explained. You will need to insert pins from the right side of the garment at the tip ends of the buttonhole; then, turn the garment to the wrong side and draw a pencil line from one pin to the other pin. With sharp, pointed scissors, cut on the pencil line; then, make diagonal slashes approximately one-fourth inch long at each corner. These edges will then be turned under and stitched with a blindstitch. (See drawing.)

If your jacket is double-breasted and the buttonholes are worked into the right front edge horizontally, your facings will have to be made of material other than grosgrain ribbon. The reason for this is that you will probably not find ribbon wide enough for your needs. You may use a firm lining material or taf-feta. Cut the facing wide enough to completely cover the over-lap of the garment, folding under the edges and hand stitching, as just explained, on each side and working around each button-

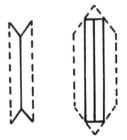

Vertical Buttonhole

hole. Make sure that you use the directional sewing to avoid shifting (see page 185).

SEWING ON BUTTONS

Buttons should be sewed to the crochet garment with split, matching yarn. Sewing thread has a different texture and the color will not match exactly. If you are using buttons with shanks and the shank is as long as the thickness of the material it must button through, you do not need to make a yarn shank. However, if the shank is not long enough, you will need to make a shank as you sew on the button. Sew the button in place, sewing through the shank three or four times, leaving a space of approximately one-eighth to one-fourth inch (depending upon how long a shank you will need) between the button and the jacket. The threads in this space will later form the yarn shank. Next, bring the needle and yarn through to the right side; wrap the yarn around the vertical threads in the space several times. Now pass the needle and yarn through to the wrong side and fasten off.

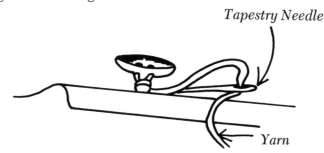

Tapestry Needle

Yarn

If you wish, a small reinforcing button may be sewed on the wrong side, directly over the stitches which will be showing from sewing your outside button. This gives your garment a more professional look. Use sewing thread to sew the "guard" buttons.

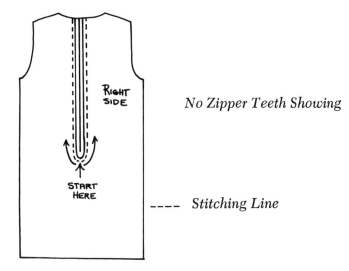

No Zipper Teeth Showing

Stitching Line

ZIPPERS

If your dress or skirt requires a zipper, work one row of single crochet around the zipper opening. Section off your work as you should do for any crochet edges (see page 173). You will want your work to lie flat and both sides to be equal. Steam the crochet edge. Pin the zipper into the opening with the two edges of crochet coming together so that *NO* zipper teeth show. It is best to work with the zipper closed. Since you are working on stretchy material, there is a great danger that the zipper teeth will become concave or that the zipper will be put in with too much fullness. To avoid either of the above, hold the zipper taut and let the material "settle" gently over the zipper. Pin it in place and then hold the skirt or dress away from you to see whether it is correct. Use sewing thread of matching color and use the backstitch, sewing from the outside of the garment. Start stitching from the very bottom of the zipper and sew toward the top edge on each of the sides to avoid shifting. (See page 166.) Make very small stitches, holding the seam *over* your finger as you sew to make sure that the zipper will not cup in. Tack the outer edge of the zipper tape into place with very small stitches, picking up a few hairs of the yarn when placing stitches on the crochet material. The skirt band will cover the upper portion of the zipper tape. The back of the neck zipper must have the upper edges turned under and stitched for a perfect finish. If the zipper is too long, it can be shortened by placing "over-and-over" stitches around the zipper chain just above the place where you want to cut it off.

BUTTON LOOPS

Most patterns for dresses or shells showing a high neckline will need an opening down the center back so that the garment will go over the head. If your dress or shell is worked in firm stitches, such as single crochet stitches, half double crochet stitches, or any other combination of stitches which does not leave large holes, you can close this opening with a neckline zipper. See instructions on page 187 for sewing in zippers. However, many patterns that use a lacy pattern stitch will not look good with a zipper closing because the heavy tape of the zipper will show through the lacy holes. It is much better in such a case to make the back neck closing using button loops and buttons. In order to finish this opening in an attractive manner, put one row of single crochet around the opening. Of course, the garment must be washed, blocked, and seamed together before the final neck edge is worked. Start at the right side of the neck opening, using the sectioning method when placing your crochet stitches. (See page 172.) Work up the other side of the opening, and then chain one stitch to turn your work around to come back down on the left side. Place one single crochet stitch in the next stitch, * chain three or four stitches, skip two stitches, single crochet in next two stitches, repeat from * to point of opening. Continue up the other side of the opening, placing one single crochet stitch in each single crochet stitch to the top.

Note: You may vary the amount of chains in the loop according to the weight of the yarn and the size of the buttons. You may also vary the amount of single crochet stitches which come between the loops; however, if the buttons are small, a most pleasing effect is achieved if the buttons are placed as close together as possible. (See drawing.)

Sew the buttons opposite the loops without making shanks, flat on the second row of single crochet. Now, work the row (rows) of edging around the neck edge.

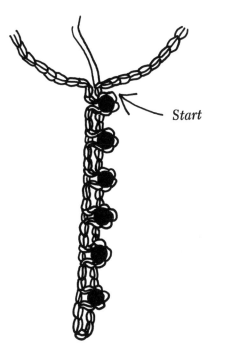

Start

9 Adapting Patterns

Changing Stitch Gauge for Different Yarns

Creating Different Sizes
How to enlarge patterns
How to make patterns smaller

Other Changes in Original Patterns

9 Adapting Patterns

CHANGING STITCH GAUGE FOR DIFFERENT YARNS

Most patterns in pattern books will suggest one kind of yarn and hook size and give you a specific stitch gauge from which to work. If the garment would be heavier or lighter in weight than you want, you can use the same patern and pattern stitch. You must, however, change the hook size and draw a new pattern of the garment for another stitch gauge. First of all, you must make little swatches of the pattern stitch in the yarn you have chosen, using several different hook sizes. Make sure that your stitch is not loose or flimsy or the finished garment will stretch considerably and will not hold its shape.

For example, assume that the yarn originally required was knitting worsted yarn, and you have found a pretty dress yarn about the weight of sport yarn that you wish to use in order to make the garment lighter in weight.

Using the following example: The gauge given in your pattern book using knitting worsted was four stitches equals one inch; five rows equals two inches. The hook size suggested was G. After trying several sizes of hooks on swatches, the decision was made to use a size O steel hook, and the gauge obtained was five and one-half stitches equals one inch; four rows equals one inch. (See photographs of both swatches.)

Swatch on Size G Hook

Swatch on Size O Hook

Note: The pattern stitch used for the swatches was:

Chain desired length of chain for foundation.

Row 1: Double crochet in second chain from hook, * sc in next ch, dc in next ch, repeat from * across row, ch 1, turn.

Row 2: Dc in first sc, * sc over next dc, dc over next sc, repeat from * across row ending last repeat dc in turning ch, ch 1, turn.

Repeat row 2 for pattern.

This pattern stitch is very simple, but it gives a lovely textured look. It is quite easy to follow the pattern because you always place a double crochet stitch over a single crochet stitch and a single crochet stitch over a double crochet stitch.

You must now choose the correct size for your measurements according to the directions given on page 33, *using the gauge given in the pattern.* After you have determined the correct size, proceed to draw a diagram, *using the gauge given in the pattern.* Then, on the same drawing, change *stitches* to inches by dividing the number of stitches by the *original gauge* (i.e., the number of stitches per inch) to get the number of inches required at all key places on the diagram.

The instructions for the jacket read:

Back: Ch 86 sts for foundation ch; work in pat st for 15″.

Shape armhole: Sl st across 5 sts, ch 1, work pat across leaving 4 sts unworked (4 sts bound off on each side). Dec 1 st each side every other row 6 times. Work even on 64 sts until 8½″ above armhole.

Shape shoulders: Bind off 7 sts at beg of next 6 rows, leaving 22 neck sts. Fasten off.

The instructions for the fronts and the sleeves are not given in words. These pieces are shown in the diagrams so that you can see just how they were to have been worked. When you are drawing your own diagrams, never change the gauge on the same drawing. Draw a separate diagram on another sheet of paper.

Study Diagram A, which shows the pattern worked out on the gauge of four stitches equals one inch, and five rows equals two inches. After the diagram was drawn, the number of stitches at each key place was changed to inches.

Diagram B shows the jacket back drawn up again using the inch measurement at each key place. Then inches were multiplied by the *new* stitch gauge of five and one-half stitches equals one inch, and four rows equals one inch. (See page 196)

Note: When making the decision on the number of stitches to bind off and decrease for the armhole, you should take the num-

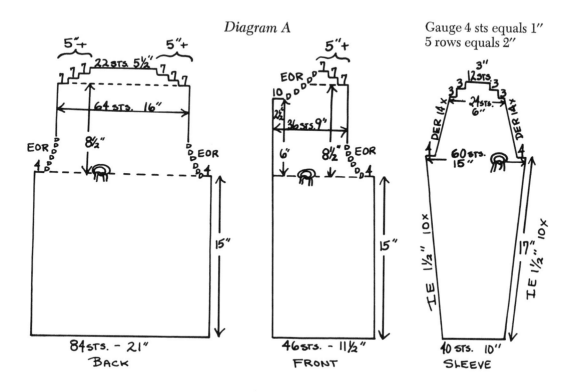

Diagram A

Gauge 4 sts equals 1″
5 rows equals 2″

ber of stitches at the bottom edge and then subtract the number
of stitches needed after the armhole decreases are taken (inch
measurement through the shoulders). By this subtraction, you
will know that you need to remove twenty-eight stitches for the
armhole shaping.

$$\begin{array}{r} 116 \text{ stitches before armhole shaping} \\ -88 \text{ stitches after armhole shaping} \\ \hline 28 \text{ stitches must come off for the armholes} \end{array}$$

Now divide the number twenty-eight by two, and take off
fourteen stitches on each side for the armhole shaping. Looking
back on the original pattern again, notice that it bound off four
stitches for the beginning of the armhole shaping, which was one
inch, since the pattern used a gauge of four stitches equals one
inch. On Diagram B, six stitches were bound off, which was the
nearest even number to one inch on the stitch gauge of five and
one-half stitches equals one inch. Then eight decreases were taken
on each side, every other row; this leaves the eighty-eight stitches

Gauge 5½ sts equals 1″
4 rows equal 1″

Diagram B

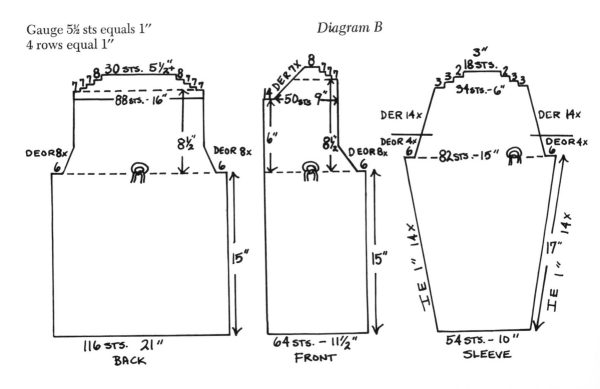

to work on for eight and one-half inches to the point of the shoulder shaping.

Carefully study the entire Diagrams A and B, making comp-parisons as you go through each step of the drawings. The row gauge of five rows equals two inches in Diagram A as compared with the row gauge of four rows equals one inch in Diagram B was considered when the sleeve cap was drawn. Notice that the distance from the bindoff row for the cap to the place where the top shaping starts is approximately five and one-half inches. The mathematics step-by-step for Diagram A (gauge—four stitches equals one inch; five rows equals two inches) looks like this:

$$
\begin{array}{l}
60 \text{ stitches before armhole shaping starts} \\
\underline{-8 \text{ stitches bound off (four stitches on each side)}} \\
52 \text{ stitches after bound-off stitches} \\
\underline{-24 \text{ after decreasing every row fourteen times}} \\
28 \text{ stitches taken off}
\end{array}
$$

The decreasing of fourteen times each side, every row, took fourteen rows.

Now divide fourteen rows by the row gauge of five rows equals two inches. You should convert the row gauge to *two and one-half rows equals one inch* for this division, and use decimals at this point.

$$
\begin{array}{r}
5.6 \\
2.5 \,)\overline{\,14.0} \\
\underline{12.5} \\
150 \\
\underline{150}
\end{array}
$$

5.6 (approximately 5½ inches from start of sleeve cap to beginning of top shaping)

When Diagram B was drawn up for the shaping of the cap of the sleeve, using the gauge of four rows equals one inch, approx-imately five and one-half inches was needed while decreasing for the cap of the sleeve. This was the same amount used for decreasing Diagram A—five and one-half inches was multiplied by four (row gauge)—therefore, twenty-two rows were needed to decrease eighteen stitches on each side.

Working mathematically through Diagram B at the sleeve cap:

$$\begin{array}{r} 82 \text{ stitches before armhole shaping starts} \\ -12 \text{ stitches bound off (four stitches on each side)} \\ \hline 70 \text{ stitches after bound-off stitches} \\ -34 \text{ stitches after decreasing} \\ \hline 36 \text{ stitches must be decreased (eighteen on each side)} \end{array}$$

$$\begin{array}{r} 4 \text{ row gauge} \\ \times 5\frac{1}{2} \text{ inches needed before top of cap of sleeve} \\ \hline 22 \text{ rows are needed} \end{array}$$

In order to decrease eighteen stitches on each side, at this point, in twenty-two rows, decreases were placed every other row four times. Then every row fourteen times on each side of the sleeve cap. In this way, you ended with twenty-two rows in all for the decreases.

This may seem a little complicated because in the example used, the stitch gauge in one diagram is not a whole number—it is five and one-half stitches equals one inch—and in the other diagram, the row gauge is not a whole number—it is, in reality two and one-half rows equals one inch. However, you may encounter many patterns dealing with stitch and row gauges which are not whole numbers, and they are all worked out in the same manner. If you work better with fractions than decimals, use fractions for your mathematics.

This pattern could have been worked out on any stitch gauge. There is one caution which must be repeated: *Never* try to change the stitch gauge right on the original diagram. *You must draw two diagrams*—the original and then the new diagram, converting to the new stitch and row gauges. You would become too con-fused if you tried to do this work all on one drawing. As a result, when you were ready to crochet from the drawing, you would run the risk of picking up the *wrong* figures (from the original gauge) instead of the new figures (from the new gauge).

If you are converting the stitch gauge on any pattern which requires you to crochet any part of the garment according to the row-wise gauge, you must figure out how far this will be in inches and how the new pattern will come out row-wise. All raglan patterns are figured row-wise, with decreases up each raglan shaping. Review pages 133–135, "Jackets with Raglan Sleeves." Adjust your new diagram of changing stitch gauge so that you will have the same raglan depth in inches that the original pattern called for.

CREATING DIFFERENT SIZES

You may need to make some garments larger than the largest size the pattern book gives, or you may need to make the garment smaller than the smallest size. This can easily be done if you are not making the garment more than several inches larger or smaller. It is not wise to make the garment a great deal larger or smaller, because you will undoubtedly run into difficulty when shaping the neck, armhole depths, sleeve widths, etc. There are pattern books available which specialize in large and extra large sizes and others which specialize in teen sizes. You should, in such a case as this, locate patterns closer to your needed mea-surements.

How to Enlarge Patterns
If the pattern you have chosen does not come in a size large enough for your needed measurements, you can enlarge the largest pattern size by an inch or two by adding more stitches to

it. You will notice from the diagrams that the sleeves are altered only slightly, because sleeves do not change in the same proportion as do the back and the fronts.

The first step in changing to a larger size is to know exactly what size you need by measuring yourself at the bust.

Example: If your actual bust is forty-one inches, the crochet size for your jacket should be forty-four inches. Next, add up all of the stitches (or patterns) given for the largest size in the pattern book for the fronts and the back at the point just before the underarm shaping as follows:

84 stitches on the back
46 stitches on one front
46 stitches on the other front
——
176 total back and fronts
−8 (deduct one overlap)
——
168 stitches at underarm

Now divide this total number of stitches by the stitch gauge of four stitches equals one inch, and you will find that the jacket size of this pattern is forty-two inches. You now know that you will need need to enlarge this pattern by about two inches (or eight stitches). You should enlarge the back piece by one inch (four stitches) and each front by one-half inch (two stitches).

Note: This is the same pattern that was used when the stitch gauge was changed from one gauge to another gauge on page 195.

Notice Diagrams A (Diagram of Large Size) and B (Diagram for Enlarging the Pattern). Diagram B was enlarged to a size 44. Changes were made at key points, such as the beginning row (from twenty-one inches to twenty-two inches on the back) and at the shoulders of the back (when the armhole stitches were taken off), from sixteen inches to sixteen and one-half inches. The

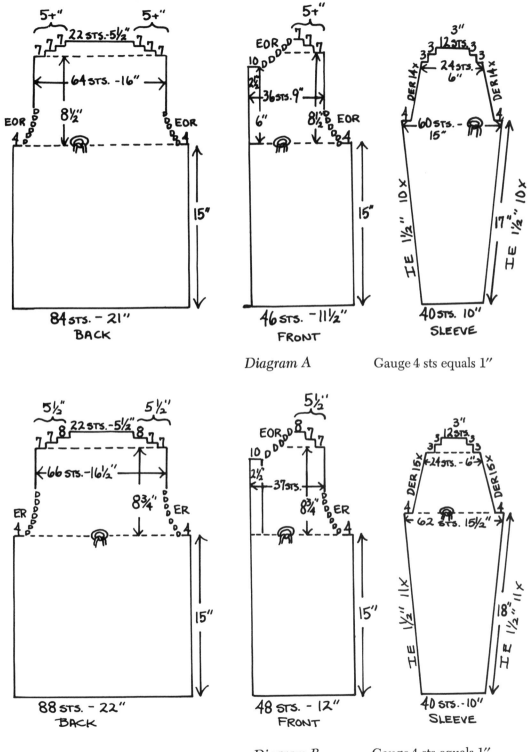

Diagram A   Gauge 4 sts equals 1″

Diagram B   Gauge 4 sts equals 1″

armhole depth was enlarged by only one-fourth inch. The fronts were enlarged from eleven and one-half inches to twelve inches on the beginning row. The width of the front shoulders on the new enlarged pattern was changed by one stitch; the neck edge remained the same. The sleeve width was enlarged by only one-half inch.

As you can see, the bottom edge and the bust measurement gained two inches in the new pattern. The armhole depth was enlarged only one-fourth inch and the shoulders were enlarged just slightly. The neck edge remained the same. The sleeves were adjusted just slightly.

How to Make Patterns Smaller

If you wish to make a pattern smaller than the smallest size by just a few inches, the procedure is the same as for making the pattern larger, except that you will be *deducting* several inches instead of *adding* on several inches. First, find out what size you will need, and then find out what size the smallest size of the pattern comes to.

Example: If the actual bust measurement is thirty-one inches, the crochet size for the jacket should be thirty-four inches. Add up all of the stitches given in the original pattern for the smallest size for the fronts and the back of the jacket just before the under-arm shaping as you were instructed to do when figuring how large the largest size was.

> 72 stitches on the back
> 39 stitches on one front
> <u>39</u> stitches on the other front
> 150 total back and fronts
> <u>−6</u> (deduct one overlap)
> 144 total stitches at bustline

Now divide the total number of stitches by the stitch gauge of four stitches equals one inch, and you will find that the jacket size of this pattern is thirty-six inches.

$$4\overline{\smash{\big)}\,144\text{ stitches}}^{\textstyle 36\text{ the size}}$$

You will need to make this pattern two inches smaller. Plan on making the back one inch smaller and each front piece one-half inch smaller.

Notice that Diagram C is the original pattern (size 36) diagrammed according to the instructions in the pattern. Then, at all the key places, stitches were changed to inches. Now notice Diagram D of the same pattern, reduced to a size 34. One inch was taken from the bottom edge of the jacket back from the original pattern and one-half inch was taken from the bottom edge of the fronts. The shoulder width was reduced by one-half inch. The

Gauge 4 sts equals 1″
7 rows equals 2″
overlap 6 sts

Diagram C

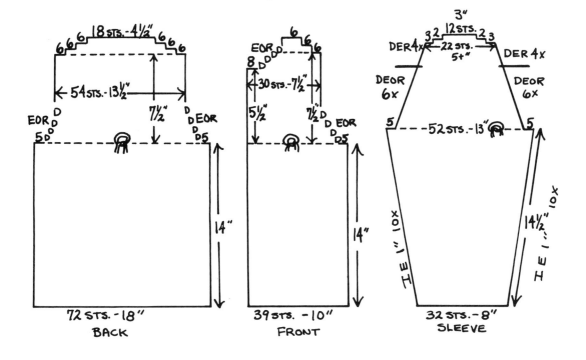

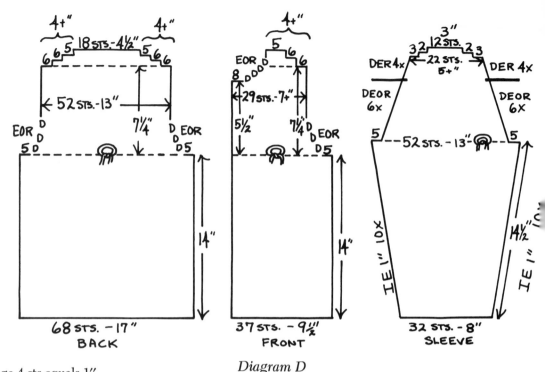

Diagram D

Gauge 4 sts equals 1″
7 rows equals 2″
overlap 6 sts

armhole depth was reduced by one-fourth inch. This left the neck shaping as it was on the original pattern. The sleeve pattern was not changed at all. A jacket sleeve measuring less than thirteen inches would be skimpy even on a small person.

OTHER CHANGES IN ORIGINAL PATTERNS

You should get into the habit of completely reading through a pattern before starting on any garment. You may want to make some changes, or perhaps you will find that the pattern needs to be adjusted to your figure.

1. If pockets are to be worked in the garment, make sure that they are positioned correctly for your figure. (See page 130.)

2. Many patterns place buttonholes according to certain numbered rows. If your pattern states, for example, to place buttonholes on the tenth row, question these instructions. You should always work the left side of the front first, and then hold the left side to your body and decide where the placement of buttons should be.

3. If you wish to raise or lower the neckline, do this on your diagram. Then when you are crocheting the front pieces, stop at the designated place where the neck shaping is to start. Hold that piece to your body to see whether you are starting the neck shaping where *you* want it. If you raise the neckline on a dress or a shell to a high neck, you will need to work a back opening for either a zipper or buttons and loops.

4. Pay particular attention to the sleeve width at the upper arm. Diagram the sleeve; then, divide the number of stitches (or patterns) by the stitch gauge so that you will know before you start the sleeve whether it is going to be too wide or not wide enough for you. Make the necessary changes directly on your diagram.

5. Carefully check the cuff measurement given in your pattern. On your diagram, change stitches (or patterns) to inches by dividing by your stitch gauge. If the sleeve bottom edge is too wide, it can be made narrower. In this case you would start out with fewer stitches or patterns. This will entail more increases on each side of the sleeve in order to arrive at the proper number of stitches or patterns required for the sleeve width at the underarm. Show all of these alterations on paper on your diagram. As you work along, keep comparing the partial pieces to your body.

10 Care and Storage of Crochet Garments

Storage

Washing and Cleaning

10 Care and Storage of Crochet Garments

STORAGE

Crochet garments, both ready-made and handmade, need special care. They should be placed in a drawer or on a shelf and never hung on coat hangers. They should be carefully folded and put away after each wearing. When folding the garments, do not make any vertical folds.

Fold a jacket by laying it out flat with the right side up, and do not button it. Now fold the sleeves over the fronts at the bustline and make one fold, bringing the bottom of the jacket up to the top. There will not be any deep creases in the jacket, because the sleeves folded over the front raises the fold. Skirts should be turned inside out. Then place several sheets of tissue paper over the skirt and make two horizontal folds in it. Dresses should also be turned inside out and folded twice over several

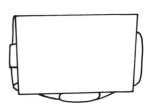

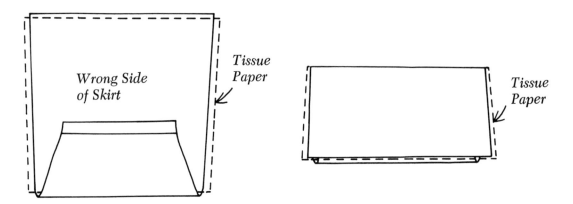

layers of tissue paper by dividing the dress into thirds. Crochet coats should never be hung on hangers. They, too, should be folded and placed on shelves or in drawers. To fold a coat, place several sheets of tissue paper over it, lay the sleeves over the front in a horizontal line, and then make *one* fold, bringing the bottom edge to the top edge. Do not place crochet garments in plastic bags. If you are storing garments on shelves, you may want to place a piece of plastic over the top of the folded garment to protect it, which will still let the garment "breathe." Never store soiled garments with clean garments.

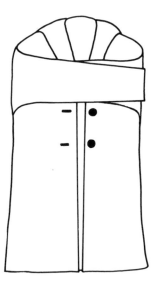

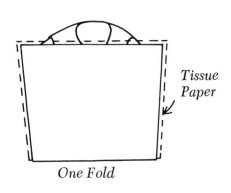

One Fold

WASHING AND CLEANING

Ready-made crochet garments should be sent to a dry-cleaning establishment. Yarns used in ready-made garments are very unpredictable. The yarn may stretch or fade; therefore, it is safer to send these garments to a good dry cleaner. Any garment (handmade or ready-made) with a lining securely attached, such as that of a coat or a jacket, will need dry cleaning instead of hand washing. All other handmade garments should be hand washed and hand blocked. Handmade dresses with linings that are attached at the neck and the armholes only may be hand washed and blocked in spite of the lining. Then, when the dress is dry, carefully press the lining.

Before washing jackets, take the following measurements:
1. Width at the bust (or chest).
2. Width at the shoulders.
3. Width at the bottom edge.
4. Width of the sleeves just before the armhole.
5. Width of the cuff.
6. Sleeve length.
7. Length of the jacket.
8. Overall length (from the back of the neck to the bottom edge).
9. Overall sleeve length (measure from the top of the cap of the sleeve to the bottom edge of the sleeve).

Take careful measurements for skirts and dresses as follows:
1. Width at the bust.
2. Width at the shoulders.
3. Width of the sleeves just before the armhole.
4. Width at the hips.
5. Width at the bottom edge.

6. Distance from the nape of the neck to the waist.
7. Distance from the waist to the bottom edge.
8. Overall skirt or dress length.
9. Overall sleeve length (measure from the top of the cap of the sleeve to the bottom edge of the sleeve).

Note: You will find that the seams tend to hold a garment together and that measurements will be much easier to take now than when you were working with the pieces of the garment before assembling.

Use the washing procedures given on page 60. Lay the jacket down flat on a padded surface. Work with the back of the jacket first, smoothing out the back as best you can, as you are working from the wrong side. Bring the back to the needed measurement (half of bust or chest measurement). Measure the length and the overall length. Make the bottom edge straight and even. Now lay the front without buttons down first, over the back, with the bottom edges even. This is done so that the buttons will not make a raised place on the buttonhole side. Then lay the other front in position, smoothing and working with all the edges so that they are straight. Carefully work with the shoulder and the neck edges—shaping and smoothing and straightening. Lay the sleeves into position, extending them straight out at each side of the jacket. Make the sleeves conform to the width and the length and the overall length measurements. Smooth out all of the wrinkles with the palms of your hands. Change the towels or padding under the garment several times to hasten the drying process.

Use the same procedures for washing and blocking dresses, skirts, or shells: measure, straighten, and smooth. You must work with the back and the front as they lie together. This is a bit difficult, as you cannot see what is going on on the wrong side.

However, when you change the towels to speed the drying process, you can take a good look at the back at that time and make any necessary corrections.

If your garment is very soiled, do not use more soap in order to get it clean. Too much soap is not good for wool and it can cause numerous problems which cannot be corrected later: matting, fading, streaking, etc. For badly soiled garments, go completely through the washing process, using the amount of soap called for on the soap package. Then, go through the same process again. After two washings, the garment should be clean. Try not to let your garments become badly soiled. When the garment gets out of shape and "elbows" and "knees" appear, it is time to wash and block, whether the garment is soiled or not.

11 Hairpin Lace

General

Learning to Make Hairpin Lace

Joining Strips of Hairpin Lace

Some Tried and True Joinings
Simple joining
Linking
Scalloped edge
Joining two strips together

Edging Strips for Trim or Insertion
Making a heading
Making outer edgings

11   Hairpin Lace

GENERAL

Originally, hairpin lace was made on real hairpins. Since this type of lace making was so tedious and time-consuming, larger hairpin lace looms were made for making these delicate strips of lace.

Hairpin lace is quite different from any other type of crochet. Delicate strands of hairpin lace may be joined in many different ways to create stoles, scarves, afghans, and dainty edge trims for garments. Using crochet threads, fancy edgings for linens may be made.

The tools used for hairpin lace are hairpin lace forks (or looms) and a crochet hook. (See photographs of two different hairpin lace forks.) The first photograph shows a one-inch fork, which is

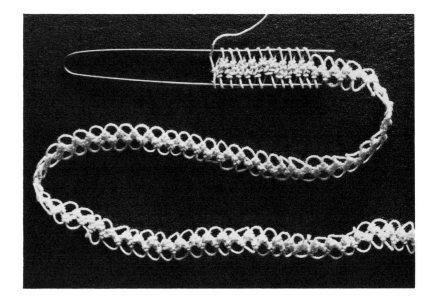

Antique Hairpin Lace

used for lightweight yarns or threads, and the second shows the newer, adjustable loom. This fork adjusts to eight different widths, ranging from one-half inch to four inches.

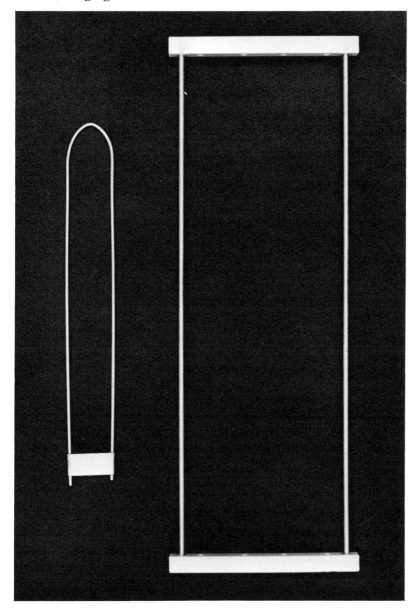

Two Hairpin Lace Forks

LEARNING TO MAKE HAIRPIN LACE

Make a slip knot on the end of the yarn; then chain one stitch. Remove the hook from the chain-one loop and place the loop on the left prong of the fork by removing the horizontal end piece.

Note: Loose yarn should be in front of the work for the *start* of hairpin lace.

Replace the end piece.

You must always hold the fork so that the bottom edge, where the removable end piece is, is pointing down and the rounded portion is in an upright position. (See drawing.) This position must be used so that you can remove loops from the bottom when the fork becomes full of loops. Put the hook back into the slip knot loop. Bring the loop on the left prong to the center between the two prongs of the fork. Place the loose thread around the right prong and hold the loose thread in back of the fork. Insert the hook into the front loop (on the left prong) and catch the loose thread and work one single crochet stitch at this position. Next, place the crochet hook in an upward position parallel to the prongs of the fork, with the hook pointing *down*, and make one turn with the fork. In turning, use clockwise rotation (the right prong comes toward you and over to the left). Bring the hook into position to the front of the work, insert the hook into the *front* loop to the *left* of center work, yarn over and work one single crochet stitch.

Note: The yarn is always in back of the work for working all stitches. Continue working in the following manner: After a single crochet stitch has been worked, put the hook into an upright position, and then turn the fork in the same direction (clockwise). Work until the loom becomes crowded, then remove the end piece and take off worked loops leaving the last four loops on each prong; then replace the base and work proceeds as before. If you are making long strips of hairpin lace, you should

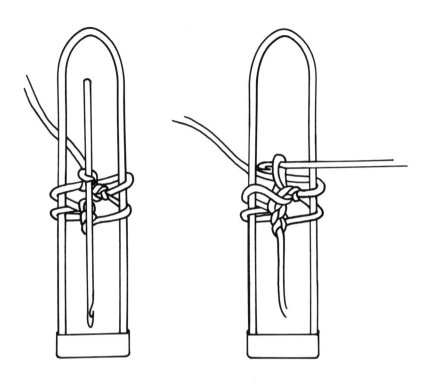

count loops and mark every twenty-fifth loop on each side of the strip until the necessary number of loops has been made. Fasten off by cutting the yarn and then pull the end yarn through the last single crochet loop.

Note: Whenever you are working hairpin lace, the loose thread is always in back of your work. The fork is always turned clockwise. The hook must be placed in an upright position between the prongs so that it may be brought to the right side of your work after each turn of the fork. The stitches you make are always in the front loop on the left side of the center work.

You may desire to try other stitches with hairpin lace. You can work almost any kind of stitch between the fork to create a different effect. You can work as just described, using a single crochet stitch, or try placing three single crochet stitches on the left thread; then, turn the fork and place three more single crochet stitches on the left thread. You may work in double crochet stitch, making two double crochet stitches in the left thread before turning the fork one turn. Try working one double crochet stitch and two treble crochet stitches in each left thread before turning the fork, or you may wish to work cluster stitches or shell stitches between the fork. This type of hairpin lace makes lovely insertion lace.

JOINING STRIPS OF HAIRPIN LACE

There are many, many ways of joining hairpin lace. The loops may be joined as they are, with no crochet between, or pretty edges may be worked through the loops of the two adjoining strips by using another thread of the same color or a contrasting color. Experiment and you may think of new ways no one else has thought of, and create an entirely different effect. When you are crocheting through these loops, you may either work with the loops untwisted or work with the loops twisted. (See drawing.)

SOME TRIED AND TRUE JOININGS

Simple Joining
Make strips of hairpin lace the length you want, and then join them by placing two strips side by side on a table, with their

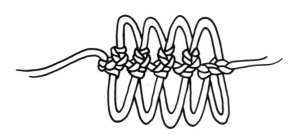
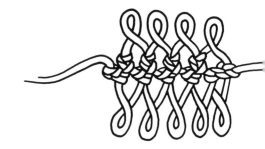

beginning edges toward you. Joining will be done with the loops twisted. (See drawing.) Attach the yarn with a single crochet stitch through the first two loops to the right of the first strip, chain three, single crochet one stitch through the first two loops to the left of the second strip, chain three, * work a single crochet stitch through the next two loops on the first strip, chain three, work a single crochet stitch through the next two loops on the second strip, chain three. Repeat from the asterisk to the top. Fasten off.

If you want a wider lacing, you may work in double crochet stitch instead of single crochet stitch. Or you may want to place shell or cluster stitches through the loops as you are joining.

Note: When you are joining with stitches through loops on the *second strip*, place your hook through from the back of the strip so that the crosses of the loops will be the same as that of the first strip.

Two Strips of Hairpin Lace Joined With Simple Joining

Linking

You may join strips together without crochet edges. The hairpin loops may be linked together to form a pretty effect for afghans, stoles, etc. All strips must have the same number of loops and they must be divisible by 3 (since you will be working through loops three at a time).

Line up on a table the first two strips to be joined, with the beginning of the two strips (where you made the slip knot and started the first loops of hairpin lace) facing you. Strips may be joined with the twist in all loops (see drawing, page 218), or you may join the loops untwisted. Do not put the strips together haphazardly. You must either decide to use twisted loops and use them throughout or use the loops untwisted. Be particular and consistent, otherwise your work will look homemade. Be on the alert and make sure that you have picked up *every* loop. Keep looking to the reverse side to see if you have missed any loops. If so, rip out your work and pick up the missing loop(s).

Two Strips of Hairpin Lace Joined By Linking

To link the joining loops, place your crochet hook through three loops on the left strip, with the hook pointing *up*; then place your hook through three loops on the right strip, with the hook pointing *up*. Pull the second three loops through the first three loops. Now pick up the next three loops on the left strip and pull these loops through the three loops already on the hook. Working from side to side continue linking until you reach the top of the strips. You may wish to link by two's—pulling two loops through two loops as just described for three loops. The resulting chain where you are connecting will be more delicate. Decide which method you like best.

Note: If you decide to use two loops, you will need an even number of loops on the strips instead of a number divisible by 3.

Since you started linking from the bottom of each strip, you can remove excess loops at the top of the strip by ripping if necessary. After all the loops have been joined and you have reached the top edge of the two strips, take needle and yarn and tack the last loop to the center hairpin work. Join all strips in the same manner. Now you are left with the side edges un-worked—there are all of the loose loops to be finished. These should be worked in a simple chain. Place your hook through three loops (or two, if you looped by twos in joining strips) and bring the next three loops through the first three loops (three loops pulled through three loops all the way to the top edge). Fasten off the last three loops by sewing them to the upper edge as you did before.

You will need to do some finishing work on the upper and lower edges. A row of single crochet stitches will give a good finish if the stitches are placed evenly. See page 170 for instructins on crocheting this edge. The top and bottom edges can then be fringed.

Scalloped Edge

These instructions are for making a hairpin lace stole. Make strips of hairpin lace the desired length in any multiple of thirty plus fifteen loops. Do not break off the yarn. Each strip will be edged and joined to the next strip as follows: Keeping all loops *twisted*, chain three, join with a slip stitch to the first chain of the chain three just made (picot), chain five, insert the hook .into the next fifteen loops on the left side, draw the loop through and work one single crochet stitch, chain three, slip stitch into the top of the single crochet stitch just made (a picot) * chain five (insert the hook into the next three loops, draw loop through and work one single crochet stitch, picot, chain five) five times. Work a single crochet stitch through the next fifteen loops, picot, repeat from * to the end of the strip. Chain five stitches, work one single crochet stitch in the *center work* of the hairpin lace (where hairpin lace was started), picot. You are now ready to start edging the opposite side of the first strip. Repeat between the * until you approach the beginning of the edging. You must end with the five groups of three loops joined, chain five, slip stitch to the beginning of edging. Fasten off.

Note: On the left side of the hairpin lace strip, the edging starts and ends with the fifteen-loop group, and on the right side of the hairpin lace strip, the edging starts and ends with the five separate groups of three loops joined. Notice that after each joining of groups of loops a picot stitch is worked. There is *always* a chain five between the joining of loops.

Joining Two Strips Together

After the second strip of hairpin lace has been made, edge one side—the left side. You will notice that the left side has the fifteen-loop groups at the top and bottom of the strip. Chain five, single crochet in the center of the bottom edge of the hairpin work, picot, chain five and start up the opposite side of the lace. Work as before for two of the five three-loop groups. You are now ready to join the *first* strip made. Place the two strips side by side on a table, with the lower edges toward you and with the first completed strip to the right of the second unfinished strip. Chain five, join the next three loops of the second strip with a single crochet stitch, chain two, remove the hook from the loop, insert the hook in the center of the picot on the *first* strip at the point where the fifteen loops were joined, pull the loop through and work a slip stitch on the second strip to finish picot. One picot has now been joined. Working on the second unfinished strip, and placing the chain fives between picots, join the second strip to the first strip at each picot as just explained. When you reach the top of the strip and have joined at the last picot, there will be two three-loop groups to work on the unfinished strip, chain five and join with a slip stitch to the center work of the hairpin lace strip where the edging started. Fasten off.

Explanation: These strips of straight hairpin lace have been made scalloped by the edging that is placed all around each strip. The first strip was edged on both sides. The second strip was edged on the left side only; then, the right side of the second strip was edged as it was joined to the first strip. You must be very careful that the joining starts in the *exact picot as stated.* By doing this correctly, the two scalloped edges will mesh together.

The photographed sample was made on a two-inch hairpin lace loom, using sport yarn. The hook size was 00 for working the hairpin lace, and 0 for the edgings and the joinings. A beautiful stole may be made by making and joining twelve strips of hairpin lace—each strip containing 435 loops. The stole should measure thirty inches wide by sixty inches long.

If you would like to make an unusual afghan, follow this same pattern on a four-inch hairpin lace loom, using knitting worsted

Two Strips of Hairpin Lace Joined With Scalloped Edge

instead of sport yarn and using larger hooks. It would be necessary to make two samples of the lace and join them together. In that way you would know how long to make the strips and how many strips would have to be made to make the afghan the size and length you wish.

There are patterns available for similar joinings, using different numbered loops. The instructions will state whether the loops are to be joined twisted or untwisted.

EDGING STRIPS FOR TRIM OR INSERTION

Lace may be edged in almost any way, either using the loops twisted or untwisted, depending upon the effect you wish to give. If you want to make a heading to be sewed to a garment, any number of headings may be used. Then the outer edge may be made plain or fancy.

Making a Heading

You may want to follow one of these methods:

1. Keeping all loops untwisted, and working through two loops at a time, attach the yarn to the first two loops and make one single crochet stitch; then make two single crochet stitches in the next two loops across. This gives a firm edge for sewing the lace to the garment.

2. Keeping all loops twisted, attach the yarn to the first three loops and work one single crochet stitch, chain three, single crochet in the next three loops, chain three. Continue across all loops to the end and fasten off.

Making Outer Edgings

A nice outer edging to go with the first heading could be made by any stitches worked through the hairpin lace loops that would keep the loops untwisted.

Example: Attach the thread in the first two loops, place one single crochet stitch in the same two loops, * chain five, slip stitch in the fourth chain from the hook (a picot made), chain one, single crochet in the next two loops. Repeat from the asterisk across.

Insertion and Heading. Example 1.

An outer edging to go with the second heading could be made by any stitches worked through the hairpin lace loops that would keep the loops twisted, and by working through them three at a time.

Example: Attach the yarn through three loops with a slip stitch, * three single crochet stitches in same place as the slip stitch, slip stitch in the next group of three loops, repeat from the asterisk across.

A wider, fancier edge containing more rows with shells or cluster stitches may used if you wish. In such a case, it is well to place the heading row on both edges of the hairpin lace; then you can work the outer edge composed of shells, clusters, etc., keeping the work flat.

Insertion and Heading. Example 2.

12 Afghan Stitch

General

Learning to Work Afghan Stitch
    Extra Tips on Afghan Stitch
    Joining new yarn
    To increase in afghan stitch
    To decrease in afghan stitch
    To bind off

Patterns in Afghan Stitch

Cross Stitching on Afghan Stitch

Colored Designs in Afghan Stitch
    To change colors

Joining Strips
    Invisible joining
    Joining by slip stitching

Working Garments in Afghan Stitch
    Assembling
        Back stitch shoulder seams
        Setting in the sleeve
        Sewing sleeve seam and side seam

12 Afghan Stitch

GENERAL

Plain afghan stitch is often used for afghans made in wide strips, or there are some patterns available for fashionable garments, such as, jackets, coats, and skirts.

Afghan stitch requires a special kind of hook, which is much longer than a regular crochet hook. Hooks are available in nine-inch and fourteen-inch lengths, and you may find flexible afghan hooks which can hold many more stitches than the usual hooks. There is no finger grip depression on afghan hooks. The shank does not taper—the thickness is the same for its entire length—and there is a knob at the end of the hook. Afghan stitch requires a longer hook because all of the stitches remain on the hook throughout the first row; then on the second row, the loops are all worked off.

LEARNING TO WORK AFGHAN STITCH

Afghan stitch is begun on a foundation chain. For practice, work a chain of twenty stitches. Work the first row as follows:

Row 1: Draw up a loop in the second chain from the hook (working through the top loop only) and in each chain of the foundation chain. Retain all of the loops on the hook. (See drawing.) You should have twenty loops on the hook.

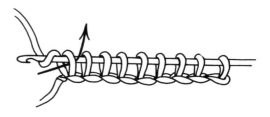

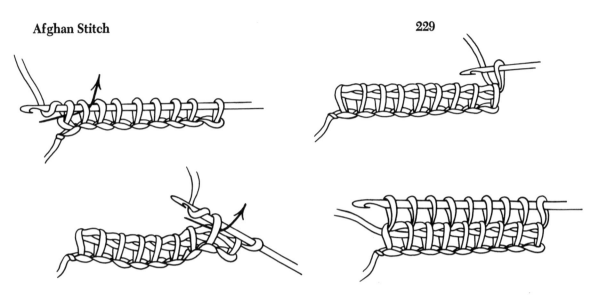

Now work the second row, which completes the stitch, as follows:

Row 2: Yarn over the hook and draw a loop through the *first* loop on the hook ° yarn over and draw a loop through *two* loops; repeat from the asterisk until one loop is left on the hook. *This last loop will count as the first stitch of the next row.* Now start again with row 1, except that you will draw up a loop in each *upright bar*, starting with the *second bar*, and retain all loops on the hook. (See drawing.) Work the second row again. This completes the stitch. (See photograph.)

Extra Tips on Afghan Stitch

1. Hold your hook "perching" your fingers on top of the shank part of the hook (see page 8, showing this hand position). The reason for using this position is because the hook is much longer and heavier than other crochet hooks and because your work becomes heavier as you proceed. This hand position can hold the extra weight much better.

2. Afghan stitch is always worked from the right side (outside). You *never* turn your work around and work back over stitches from the opposite side of the work (wrong side).

3. The stitches will look quite different on the wrong side of the work.

4. Always start back on the second row by doing the following: yarn over hook and pull a loop through *one* loop; then the loops are worked off by yarn over and pull a loop through *two* loops for the rest of the row, ending with *one* loop left on the hook. This is the first stitch for the next row.

5. Maintain the count of twenty stitches on each and every row.

6. Practice long enough before starting a project so that your work is even. Many people learning this stitch will either tighten

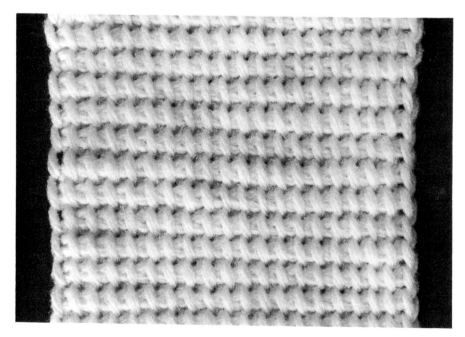

Afghan Stitch

or loosen their stitches; then the piece will be wider or narrower in places. Learn to keep the same tension on the yarn to even your stitches. Measure your sample width-wise in several places to see if you are working evenly.

7. When pattern books direct you to work a certain number of rows in afghan stitch, this means the number of *completed* rows—which takes two rows to complete. The first row is to pick up loops and the second row is to work off the loops.

Joining New Yarn

When it is time to add new yarn, add it on the *second* row (the row in which you are working off the loops two at a time). Do not knot the yarn; simply lay in the new strand and pull it through two loops. All ends should fall to the wrong side of your work so they can be worked in later. The ends worked in would be much more conspicuous if you should add the new yarn on the first row (the row in which all the loops are picked up and retained on the hook). If you come upon a knot in the yarn as it unwinds from the ball, it must be cut out and a new strand started as just explained.

To Increase in Afghan Stitch

Your pattern for garments will require increases on each side of certain pieces to make the piece wider, for example, sleeves. Since sleeves are started at the cuff, gradual tapering takes place to widen the sleeve. The increases are always placed on the first row of afghan stitch (the row in which loops are picked up and retained on the hook). To increase at the beginning of the row, pick up a loop in the *first* upright bar. Ordinarily this first bar is

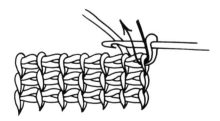

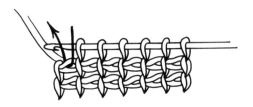

skipped. This gives an extra stitch at the right edge of your work. In order to increase at the other end of the work (the left side), you must pick up a loop between the last two upright bars; then pick up a loop in the last upright bar.

Note: When working the increased stitch at the end of the row, do not place the hook in the entire space between the last two bars. This would leave a large unsightly hole. Pick up the new extra stitch through the top part of the chain between the last two bars. (See drawing.) Count the number of loops on the hook to make sure that you have the necessary number of stitches *after each increase row*.

To Decrease in Afghan Stitch

A decrease in afghan stitch is worked as follows: One stitch is decreased at each end of the row. At the right end of the work, the first and second stitches are joined (draw up a loop in the second bar as usual, then bring this loop through the first loop);

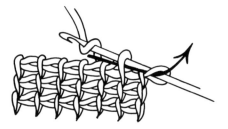

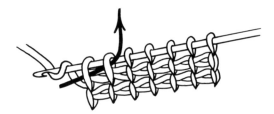

then the row is continued as usual to the end of the row. On the return row, the decrease is made at the left end of the work as follows: Yarn over and pull a loop through *two* loops (instead of the usual *one* loop for the first stitch on the return row); then finish the row as usual. Count the number of stitches to make sure that you are maintaining the number needed *after* the decrease row.

To Bind Off

When the completing row of afghan stitch is worked (the second row in which the loops are taken off the hook), the piece is actually bound off. However, the edge is not considered finished without a last row of single crochet or slip stitch worked into each stitch. This firms the top edge and eliminates holes. Work one row of slip stitch by placing the hook into the upright bar. Or, work a single crochet stitch in each upright bar. (See drawing.)

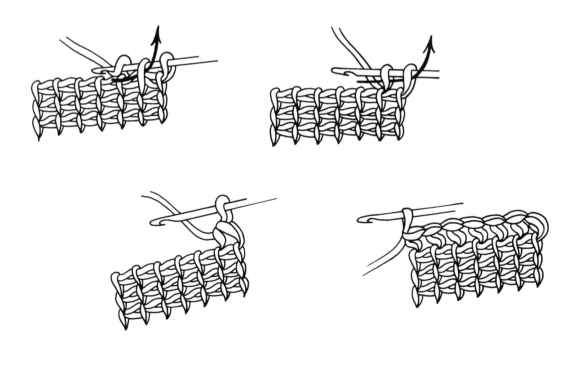

PATTERNS IN AFGHAN STITCH

Many different pattern stitches may be worked in afghan stitch, for example, purl stitches, cross stitches, yarn overs, etc. Embossed effects may be created by working into rows below. Your pattern will state how the stitches are to be worked if plain afghan stitch is not to be used.

CROSS STITCHING ON AFGHAN STITCH

Patterns for cross stitch on afghan stitch will include a chart to follow for the embroidery and a key to the colors used. The chart will explain where to place the design. Each square on the chart represents one stitch in afghan stitch. You should sew a basting line with sewing thread to divide the strips into sections. This will help you center the design. Cross stitch should always be done with threads crossing in the same direction. If several stitches are to be worked with one color on the same row, work the first half of each cross stitch across the row and then come back from the opposite direction to complete the row. Cross stitch over afghan stitch should not show on the wrong side. If you place your stitches carefully, the needle can pass through the thickness of the work without coming through to the wrong side. Do not use knots to start and end strands; weave them carefully

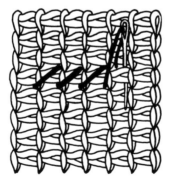
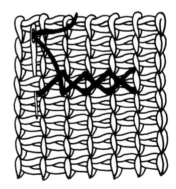

between the thickness and then clip off. Practice working cross stitch on a sample of afghan stitch. Bring the needle through the work from the wrong side (leave an end of approximately four inches) to the bottom and to the left of the upright bar you wish to cover with a cross stitch. Now pass the needle behind the two horizontal threads, with the needle pointing down on the right side of the same bar, and pull the yarn through. Make sure that the needle is not coming through to the wrong side—the needle should pass behind the two horizontal threads *only*. Work the next stitch as just explained. After the first half of the cross stitch has been completed (for the group of stitches to be worked with the same color), finish the crosses by placing the needle in the same place where the needle was placed for the first half of the cross.

Caution! Do not pull the stitches too tightly. The stitches must just "sit" on top of the work for best results.

Cross Stitch on Afghan Stitch

COLORED DESIGNS IN AFGHAN STITCH

Designs may be worked in color in afghan stitch. Such afghans are usually made in one piece. Since the number of stitches involved will no doubt be large, the stitches will be quite crowded on the hook. As previously mentioned, there are flexible afghan hooks available in some parts of the country and through needlecraft mail order companies. These hooks have two advantages—they are flexible and they hold a great many more stitches than the fourteen-inch afghan hooks. However, you can use two fourteen-inch afghan hooks if the stitches are crowded. Start working stitches with the second hook at approximately the halfway point. This is a little more awkward than using a flexible hook, but easier than trying to use just the one hook. When the stitches are very crowded, one has a tendency to make uneven stitches.

A chart is furnished with the pattern and also a key to symbols used for colors. Read the chart from the bottom to the top and from right to left. One square on the chart indicates one stitch of afghan stitch. Remember that it takes two rows to complete one row of afghan stitch.

To Change Colors

Work the specified number of loops for the beginning row of afghan stitch (the row in which you pick up loops and retain them on the hook) with the first color. Then, taking the second color, pick up the designated number of loops with the second

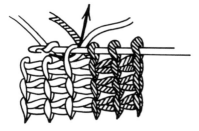

Picking up Loops

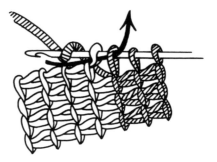

Working off Loops

color. If the first color is to be used again, with no more than three stitches between, you should carry the yarn loosely across the back of the work until needed again. If more than three stitches are to be worked before the first color is needed again, you should use another ball of the first color. Add balls of colors for each new color change.

On the second row of afghan stitch (the row in which the loops are worked off), work off the loops with the matching color until *one* loop remains before the second color. Then take up the second color from underneath the first color. This twists the colors to prevent holes. The second color will be worked through two loops—one loop of the first color and one loop of the second color. Add new colors as needed, and cut off colors no longer needed, leaving approximately four-inch ends, which will be worked in on the wrong side.

Colored Designs in Afghan Stitch

Note: It can be quite distressing if you are working an elaborate pattern where many colors are used and there are many balls of colors attached to the afghan. This situation can be helped to a degree. In order to alleviate the tangle of balls of yarn, in areas where little patches of colors appear or where lines of one color are to be worked, count the number of squares used in the patches or lines. Then cut a strand of that color long enough to work the specified number of stitches. Cut the strand, allowing approximately two inches for each square on the chart, plus an allowance of four inches at each end for working in the ends. Medium-size patches of color may be wound on knitting bobbins. For the larger patches or background work, you will need to use balls of yarn.

These afghans are so lovely when finished, it is worth the effort and the entanglement!

Carefully wash and block the finished afghan before adding fringe. See page 300 for directions on tying fringe.

JOINING STRIPS

Strips of afghan stitch may be joined in a number of ways. Your pattern will suggest a way, or you may use either of the two ways explained below.

Invisible Joining

You may wish to make an invisible joining of two strips that will not leave a ridge on the right side of your work. This method of joining should be used whenever the pattern suggests whipping edges together because it looks much more professional. If the strips to be joined are different colors, after you have mastered the technique of joining, you should experiment on a sample, first sewing with one color and then another to determine which color is the least conspicuous. Split yarn must be used.

Notice that the two side edges of a strip of afghan stitch do not look alike. On the right edge of afghan stitch you will notice a nice firm chain edge, and on the left edge of the same strip, the edge looks a little ragged and more open. When you join two strips together, you will not want an entire chain edge to show, nor will you want the ragged edge to show. You will want the finished seam to look like *one "bar"* of afghan stitch. You must therefore conceal one-half of the chain and the entire ragged edge.

Line up the two strips with the top edge uppermost. You will sew from the top to the bottom of the strips (starting at the bound-off edges), matching rows. The edges to be joined will be a chain edge on the first strip to the left of the seam and a ragged edge to the right of the seam. Join the yarn to the top of the first strip without a knot and make a "tack" stitch at the very top edge of strip number one. Now take a little tack stitch at the very top edge of the second strip. Then, working from side to side, take a small stitch through the *center* of the chain edge on the first strip, with the needle running parallel to the edge. Now take a stitch on the second strip, with the needle running parallel to the edge, picking up *two horizontal threads* lying to the *left* of the first perfect bar. With your thumbnail, push the resulting seam to the wrong side of the work. Working from side to side repeat the process, first stitching into the center of the chain edge on the first strip, then picking up the two horizontal threads on the second strip. (See drawing.)

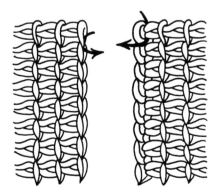

Joining Two Strips of Afghan Stitch—Invisible Joining

Joining Two Strips of Afghan Stitch—Slipstitching

Note: With each stitch you take, the needle must always point down. Stretch the seam just slightly after approximately three sets of joining stitches. This eliminates the danger of the thread eventually breaking or the seam puckering.

Joining by Slip Stitching
Line up the two strips to be joined with the bound-off edges together and with the right sides out and the wrong sides touching each other. You should work from the top to the bottom of each strip. Attach the yarn to the very top bound-off stitches of each piece. Draw a loop through and make one chain stitch. This joins the two strips together. Now slip stitch both strips together through the side stitches, matching rows. This will form a pretty ridge on the *right* side of the work. Work all strips together as for the first, starting at the top and working down.

Note: When the two strips are lined up ready to be joined with the row of slip stitches, the strip with the ragged edge will be facing you and the strip with the chain edge will be directly opposite and on the wrong side. Place your hook through the thread on the ragged edge and through the entire chain of the other strip. (See photograph.)

WORKING GARMENTS IN AFGHAN STITCH

There are some patterns available for jackets, skirts, dresses, etc., that use afghan stitch. These garments are usually quite heavy; therefore, a little more allowance is needed than you would ordinarily add. The heavier the garment the more allowance you need. (See pages 33–36, Choosing the Correct Size.)

Use all methods previously mentioned: working an accurate stitch gauge, drawing the diagrams, counting rows on like pieces (or pieces which will be joined together), blocking the partial pieces, blocking the finished pieces, and basting the garment together for a fitting.

Assembling

Garments which have been worked in afghan stitch must have careful attention as to finishing. Since the pieces are quite thick, seams must be carefully sewed and steamed. These garments assemble nicely using knitting assembly techniques. Do not place seams side-by-side and sew them on the very edge. This will result in a garment with a very "homemade" look. Joggy, uneven edges cannot be made straight. Such an example is the cap of the sleeve, or any other area where decreases and bind-offs are placed. For best results use back stitching on uneven edges and invisible joining on side edges which do not have any increases or decreases.

Before you start seaming the pieces together, examine all bind-off areas. Every bound off edge containing more than two stitches must have a finish of slip stitching. Inspect all pieces of your garment at the left side edges. All bound off edges at the left will not have a finish of slip stitching. Attach yarn and work slip stitching across these portions of bound off stitches.

Note: You will recall that when you were crocheting these pieces, and you were shaping for the underarm (as an example), you were to have slip stitched across 6 stitches and then worked in afghan stitch to within 5 stitches of the end of the row. This binds off 5 stitches at each end of the piece. The bind-off on the right end is finished with slip stitch, but the other end (the left end) of the piece is not finished with slip stitching. These little places will need slip stitching in each stitch—otherwise deeper seams must be made to hide the holes which are present. This involves all bind-offs at the underarm, shoulders, neck edges, and any other bind-offs containing more than two stitches.

BACK STITCH SHOULDER SEAMS

Before commencing to sew your garment together, review back stitching and notice the drawing of the stitch on page 166. Use strands of split yarn for neater, smaller seams. Back stitched seams are worked from the wrong side; therefore, pin the shoulders together with the wrong sides out. Start stitching from the armhole and work toward the neck edge. Make your stitches very close together. Taper the stitching line—do not jog. From time to time, examine the seam from the right side of your work to make sure your "vertical bar" afghan stitches are matching at the seam. This gives a more professional look. Make sure that NO bound off edges show from the finished side. To avoid this, you must not sew on the very edge. The stitching line must be set in approximately one-fourth inch from the edge. Steam the seam with the "wet wash cloth" method, and then open the seam by pressing gently with your fingers.

SETTING IN THE SLEEVES

Notice that on the back and fronts of your jacket at the armhole, you have a bound-off edge, then a curve (made by decreases), and then a long straight line up to the shoulders. You will want a long straight line showing; therefore, do not sew in the sleeve haphazardly. A sleeve set in with the seam wiggling in and out of rows at the long straight line area can certainly ruin the best crocheted garment. You must plan on setting in the sleeve in such a way that the seam will be straight, exposing the second vertical bar all the way up the straight line. Put in a guide line with a contrasting color thread or fine yarn from the right side of your work just to the side of the vertical bar you wish to expose. Place this guide line, which is like a basting thread, with stitches quite close together on all of the straight line edges of the back and fronts of the jacket (make sure the guide line stitches show on the wrong side). All guide lines must follow through the shoulder seam and onto the other side of the armhole without a jog.

You are now ready to pin in the sleeve. Hold your work so that the jacket is facing you, not the sleeve. You will want to be able to see the guide line you placed on the straight line edges, and should you be sewing from the sleeve side you could not see the guide line. Find the center of the cap of the sleeve by folding the sleeve in half and inserting a pin at the center point. Pin this center pin to the shoulder seam with wrong sides out. Place pins all around the armhole, easing in any fullness.

Note: When pinning in the sleeve, allow the sleeve to extend beyond the armhole of the jacket by a very slight degree. Since there are decreases and bind-offs on the sleeve caps, the sleeves will set in nicer if they are not seamed quite so close to the edge.

Start seaming from the bound-off underarm edge. Use the back stitch and place your stitches very close together. Place your stitching line in far enough so that the unevenness of the bind-offs and decreases does not show (approximately one-fourth inch) from the right side. When you approach the long straight line area, place your back stitches ever so carefully by following the guide line. Examine your stitching from the right side from time to time, so that you can remove any stitches which do not please you.

After the seaming has been completed, steam the armhole seams, taking many little steps to get around the curves without stretching the pieces in any other place. Open the seams as before.

SEWING SLEEVE SEAM AND SIDE SEAM

Pin the sleeve with the right sides together so that the rows match, and sew the seam with a back stitch approximately one-fourth inch from the edge. Take very small stitches, starting at the cuff edge and working toward the underarm edge. Do not fasten off the yarn when the seam is completed. Bring the needle and yarn through to the right side of your work, and sew the side seam using the invisible joining seam, following instructions given on page 238. Carefully steam the seams.

For finishing details see page 169.

13 Medallions

General

Working Medallions
Working a sample medallion
Square medallions
   Granny squares
   Small square
   Lacy square
Hexagonal medallions
   Small hexagon
   Roll stitch hexagon
Sunburst medallion

Joining Medallions
Example of joining with fancy edging
Joining by slip stitching
Joining by sewing
Joining at picots

Working Half Medallions

Other Methods of Starting Medallions

Diagrams for Medallion Garments
Example diagram

Japanese Symbols
Example diagrams in Japanese symbols

Other Uses for Medallions
Combining medallions with fabrics
Rugs
   Hexagonal medallion rug
   Square medallion rug
Wall hangings and pictures

13 Medallions

GENERAL

Medallion patterns can be used to make tablecloths, bedspreads, doilies, rugs, and most any kind of garment. A medallion is a complete unit in itself. It may be joined together with other medallions in a variety of ways to make the above items. There are lovely patterns to choose from. They may be found in old and new crochet books featuring doilies, tablecloths, and spreads.

If you wish to make garments using yarns and medallions, just select the center part of any pattern for tablecloths, spreads, or doilies. If you are using a lightweight yarn, such as a fingering yarn or a sport yarn, and you are trying to achieve a delicate look, an average number of rounds to work would be about three to twelve. Or the medallions may contain many more rounds, depending upon the type of garment and your own desires. If you have not made medallions before, experiment with yarns of different weights and textures and try different size hooks. You will be amazed at the beauty and simplicity of medallions. They may be joined in so many ways that it would be impossible to ever describe all of them. You may think up joinings that no one else has ever thought of before. They can be joined so that the medallions are touching each other, or they can have wide and fancy joinings of the same color or a contrasting color.

There are Japanese crochet pattern books available which show these lovely medallion patterns joined together to form most any kind of garment. Many of the patterns in these books are shown in color so that you can see how the finished garments will look. Japanese pattern books are available in this country and can be purchased at Japanese bookstores in the larger cities. The Japanese books use symbols to represent the various stitches, and you can learn to read the symbols and use their beautiful patterns without the knowledge of the Japanese language. Some examples using the symbols will be shown in this book. They are not, however, copied from any Japanese book but are adaptations of the author's which originally were given in words.

WORKING MEDALLIONS

Medallions are started in the center and they are worked in *rounds* instead of in rows (where you would work across a row, then turn your work around and work back from the opposite direction). When you come back to the starting place, a round has been completed. The right side of your work is facing you. Many patterns start the center, with a chain of a specified number of stitches, and then the chain is joined to form a circle by placing a slip stitch in the first chain made. The pattern will then commence the rounds. Increases will be placed evenly so that the medallion lies flat. Your pattern will state exactly *how* and *where* the increased stitches are to be made. The increases may be part of a petal or a shell that has more stitches than the previous round. The finished medallions may be round, square, hexagonal (six-sided), or octagonal (eight-sided).

Working a Sample Medallion Step-by-Step

The instructions for the sample medallion are from an old bedspread pattern. This lovely pinwheel pattern has been used over and over again with variations for all sorts of trims, centers of doilies, and garments of all types. The instructions include only the first fourteen rows.

Instructions for the sample medallion read:
Ch 4, join with a sl st to form a ring.
Rnd 1. 12 sc in ring.
Rnd 2. Sc in 1st sc, * ch 3, sk next sc, sc in next sc; repeat from * 5 times more, (6 ch-3 loops.)
Rnd 3. Sc in ch-3 lp, * ch 3, sc in next sc, sc in ch-3 lp; repeat from * 4 times more, ch 3, sk next sc, sc in next sc.
Rnd 4. 2 sc in ch-3 lp, * ch 3, sk next sc, sc in next sc, 2 sc in ch-3 lp; repeat from * 4 times more, end ch 3, sk next sc, sc in each of next 2 sc.
Rnd 5. 2 sc in ch-3 lp, * ch 3, sk next sc, sc in each of next 2 sc, 2 sc in ch-3 lp; repeat from * 4 times more, end ch 3, sk next sc, sc in each of next 3 sc.
Rnd 6. 2 sc in ch-3 lp, * ch 3, sk next sc, sc in each of next 3 sc, 2 sc in ch-3 lp; repeat from * 4 times more, end ch 3, sk next sc, sc in each of next 4 sc. Continue in this manner until there are 13 sc sts in each spoke of pinwheel. Fasten off.

Explanation: Chain four stitches, then the chain is joined to form a circle by placing a slip stitch in the first chain. (See drawing.) The rounds now start.

For round 1, make twelve single crochet stitches in the ring. The stitches are placed through the *entire ring*—not into the separate chain stitches. (See drawing.)

Joining into a circle by a slip stitch   *Stitches placed through the entire ring*

The rounds are not joined with a slip stitch in this particular pattern. You can tell when you have finished a round if you count stitches as you go along.

Before starting round 2, it must be explained that the pattern writer is using asterisks for repeats instead of parenthesis; therefore, the work between the asterisks is to be done six times. Also, keep in mind that because medallions are worked in rounds and not in rows (as has been previously explained on page 13), the right side of your work is always facing you. When you are ready to place your hook into a stitch in the round previously worked, the hook is placed just to the *right* of the stitch (instead of to the *left* of the stitch, as you would when working in rows). (See drawing.)

For round 2, start with a single crochet stitch in the first single crochet stitch (in the round below), and then do the work between the asterisks *six times*. You should then have six chain-three loops.

For round 3, start by working a single crochet stitch in the chain-three loop of the previous round; then the work between the asterisks is worked five times, ending with chain three, skip the next single crochet stitch, and single crochet in the next single crochet stitch. You are now around to the starting place, with the start of six spokes to the pinwheel. These spokes gradually become wider and wider, as more and more rounds are worked.

Note: When working this medallion for the first time, count your stitches on each round. Then you will know when you are back to the starting place again.

On round 3, you will have two single crochet stitches in each spoke of the pinwheel—therefore, twelve single crochet stitches in all.

On round 4, you will have three single crochet stitches in each spoke—therefore, in all you will count eighteen single crochet stitches.

Sample Medallion—Pinwheel

On round 5, you will have four single crochet stitches in each spoke and twenty-four single crochet stitches.

On round 6, you will have thirty single crochet stitches (five in each spoke).

Continue round after round until each spoke contains thirteen single crochet stitches, and then fasten off. See the completed hexagonal (six-sided) medallion.

Square Medallions

Most of the square medallions start in the center with a circle. The medallions may remain round for a number of rounds before the corners that square them off are started. The examples given in this text are just a sample of hundreds of different square medallions available in pattern books. Perhaps you can make up some designs of your own with a little experimentation.

Granny squares (where colors are changed on each round) were originally made into afghans for the purpose of utilizing leftover yarns. However, these colorful little squares are finding new popularity since there are many patterns available in pattern books, showing how to join the squares to make coats, scarves, jackets, and skirts—even ponchos!

GRANNY SQUARES

Ch 5, join with a sl st to form ring.

Rnd 1. Ch 3, 2 dc in ring (ch 1, 3 dc in ring) 3 times, end ch 1, join with a sl st in 3rd ch of turning ch. Fasten off 1st color.

Rnd 2. Join 2nd color in any ch-1 sp, ch 3, 2 dc in same sp, * 3 dc, ch 1, 3 dc in next ch-1 sp; repeat from * 2 times more, ending 3 dc, ch 1 in starting ch-1 sp. Join with a sl st to top of ch 3. Fasten off 2nd color.

Rnd 3. Join 3rd color in any ch-1 sp, ch 3, 2 dc in same sp, * 3 dc in space between next two 3 dc group; in next ch-1 sp work 3 dc, ch 1, 3 dc (a corner made), repeat from * two times, ending 3 dc in space between next two 3 dc group; 3 dc, ch 1 in starting ch-1 sp. Join with a sl st to top of ch 3. Fasten off 3rd color.

Continue changing colors and working 3 more rounds as established by working 3 dc, ch 1, 3 dc in corners and on the sides of squares, work 3 dc between each 3 dc group.

Explanation: The granny square is started in the center, as usual, with chain stitches joined into a ring. The corners of the square are started on the first round. The first corner is not completed until the end of the round. In each corner you must work three double crochet stitches, chain one, and three double crochet stitches. When you come back around to the starting place, you will work three double crochet stitches, chain one and join to the top of the beginning chain. This completes the first corner. (See photograph.)

Notice the second photograph. This is the same granny square pattern worked out with two colors. Both colors are worked on each round after the first two rounds are worked with the first color. The color *not in use* is carried loosely behind the work and worked in along the base of the stitches, then taken up again when needed. The corners are all worked in the first color and the "between" three double crochet groups are worked with the second color.

Note: When changing colors, the last step of the double crochet stitch is always worked with the new color, and the colors are twisted on the wrong side of the work to prevent holes.

SMALL SQUARE MEDALLION

Ch 5, join with a sl st to form ring.

Rnd 1: Ch 6, * 3 dc in ring, ch 3, repeat from * 2 times more, end rnd by 2 dc, join with a sl st to 3rd chain of first ch 6 (4 3-dc groups).

Rnd 2: * Sc in ch-3 sp, ch 4, sc in same sp, (corner made); ch 3, repeat from * around; join with a sl st.

Rnd 3: * Sc in corner sp; in same sp make (1 hdc, 2 dc, ch 3, 2 dc, 1 hdc, 1 sc); in center ch of next ch-3, place a group of 1 dc, ch 1, 1 dc, ch 1; repeat from * around. Join with a sl st and fasten off.

Explanation: This square medallion is started in the center with a small chain and it is joined to form a circle. The corners

Granny Square

Second Granny Square

Small Square Medallion

are started on the second round and the third round finishes it off. This small medallion could be worked in heavier yarns for different effects. There are many possible uses for small medallions. They could be made of several colors, such as pink, blue, and yellow (alternating the colors on each separate medallion), and joined with white for children's garments. A string of them could be used as strips of trim on almost any garment. A pretty belt could be made from them.

LACY SQUARE MEDALLION

Ch 8, join with a sl st to form a ring.

Rnd 1: Work 12 sc in ring, join with a sl st in first sc of rnd.

Rnd 2: Ch 5, work a tr in joining st, 1 more tr in same place, ch 3, sl st in 4th st from hook (picot), * ch 5, sk 2 sts in ring, work a tr in next st, ch 3, picot, 4 more tr in same place, ch 3 picot; repeat from * 2 times more, end with ch 5, sk 2 sts, 1 tr in joining st below, ch 3, picot, 1 more tr in same place, join with a sl st in top st of ch 5 at beg of rnd.

Rnd 3: Ch 5, work 2 tr in same place as joining st below, * ch 3, picot, ch 7, picot, ch 2, 1 sc in space, ch 6, picot, ch 3, 1 tr in top of center tr of next group of 5 below, ch 3, picot, 4 more tr in same place; repeat from * around ending with ch 6, picot, ch 3, 1 tr in joining st of rnd below, ch 3, picot, 1 more tr in same place; join with a sl st in top st of chain 5 at beg of rnd.

Rnd 4: Ch 8, work * 1 sc in next sp, ch 5, sk next 2 picots, 1 sc in next sp, ch 5, 1 dc in top of center tr of group of 5 trebles below, ch 4, 1 dc in same place, ch 5; repeat from * around, end with 1 sc in next sp, ch 5, sk next 2 picots, sc in next sp, ch 5, dc in center tr of group of 5 tr below, ch 4, join with a sl st to 3rd ch of beg ch 8.

Rnd 5: Ch 1, work 6 sc in each ch-5 sp around. Join with a sl st.

Rnd 6: Ch 1, 1 sc in joining st, 1 sc in each of next 3 sc, ch 3, picot, sc in next 6 sts, * picot, sc in next 6 sts, repeat from * to last corner space, ch 3, picot, sc in next 3 sts. Join with a sl st in first st of rnd and fasten off.

Explanation: This square medallion has a delicate lacy look—it could be used for a shell, a shawl, or a pretty cardigan. There should be no difficulty in reading the instructions with the exception of working the picot. In some instances, the picot stitch is worked next to a treble crochet stitch. In the middle of the chain loops on round 3, where the instructions read, "ch 7, picot," a slip stitch is placed in the *fourth* stitch from the hook on the chain seven just made. (See photograph.)

Hexagonal Medallions

SMALL HEXAGON

Ch 6, join with a sl st to form ring.

Rnd 1: Ch 3, 17 dc in ring, join with a sl st to top of first ch 3.

Rnd 2: Ch 6, dc in same st as joining, * ch 2, skip 2 sts, dc in next st, ch 3, dc in same st, repeat from * around ending ch 2, skip 2 sts, join with a sl st to 3rd ch of first ch 6 (6 ch-3 spaces).

Rnd 3: Sl st under next ch-3 lp, ch 3, 6 dc in same lp, * ch 1, skip next dc, next ch-2 lp, and next dc; 7 dc in next ch-3 lp; repeat from * around, ending ch 1, join with a sl st to top of first ch 3.

Rnd 4: Ch 4, dc in next dc, ch 1, dc in next dc, * ch 1, tr in next dc (corner), (ch 1, dc in next dc) 6 times. Repeat from * around ending ch 1, tr in next dc, (ch 1, dc in next dc) 3 times; ch 1, join with a sl st to 3rd ch of first ch 4. Fasten off.

Explanation: These instructions just quoted use both parentheses and asterisks. (Review pages 72–74.) The pattern writer is always referring to the placement of stitches in the round just worked. At times she states to place the next stitch in a double crochet stitch, for example, and at other times she just states to place the stitch in the next "stitch." There are six treble crochet

Lacy Square Medallion

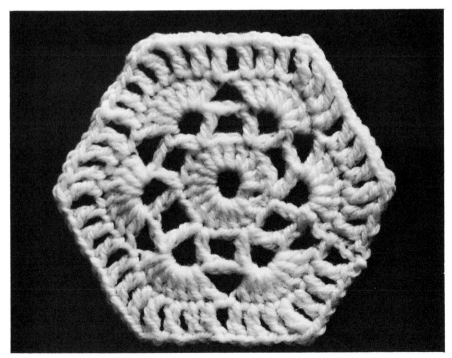

Small Hexagon Medallion

stitches on the fourth round and they are the six points of the hexagon.

This small hexagonal medallion may be joined with sides touching, or a pretty joining edge may be worked. It would be suitable for most any type of garment, in one color or several colors. If the yarn is heavy, the last row may be omitted without detracting from the looks of the medallion.

ROLL STITCH HEXAGON

Ch 6, join with a sl st to form a ring.

Rnd 1: Ch 3, 15 roll sts (thread over 15 times) in ring, join with a sl st.

Rnd 2: Ch 5, * 1 dc in next roll st, ch 2; repeat from * around ending with a sl st in 3rd st of first ch 5.

Rnd 3: Sl st in next lp, ch 3, 2 dc in same lp, holding back last loop of each dc on hook, yarn over and work off all lps (1 cluster made). * Ch 1, cluster in next dc (cluster st: 3 dc in same st, holding back last lp of each dc on hook, yarn over and work off all lps), ch 1, cluster in next space; repeat from * around, ending cluster in last dc, ch 1, join with a sl st to top of 1st cluster.

Rnd 4: * Sc in next ch-1 sp, ch 3, sc in next ch-1 sp, ch 3, sc in next ch-1 sp, ch 4, sl st in 3rd ch from hook (picot), ch 1, sc in next ch-1 sp, ch 3, sc in next ch-1 sp, ch 3, sc in next ch-1 sp, ch 3, sl st in top of last sc made (picot), repeat from * around. Join with a sl st and fasten off.

Explanation: Be sure to practice making roll stitches before starting this medallion. See page 185. These beautiful medallions may be used for most any garments. They join nicely through the picots on the last row.

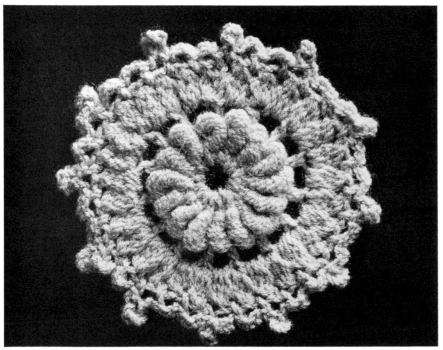

Roll Stitch Medallion

Sunburst Medallion

Sunburst Medallion

Ch 5, join with a sl st to form ring.

Rnd 1: Ch 1, * sc in ring, ch 1; repeat from * around, join with a sl st. (12 ch-1 spaces.)

Rnd 2: Sl st in next sp, ch 6, (dc in next ch-1 sp, ch 3) 11 times. Join to 3rd ch of beg ch 6.

Rnd 3: Sl st in next sp, ch 4, 3 tr in same space, holding back the last lp of each tr on hook; yarn over and draw through all lps on hook, ch 1 to fasten (a cluster). * Ch 4, 4 tr in next sp, holding back last lp of each tr on hook, yarn over and draw lp through all lps on hook, ch 1 to fasten cluster; repeat from * around, ch 4, join to top of 1st cluster.

Rnd 4: Ch 6, * sc in next sp, ch 3, dc in top of next cluster, ch 3; repeat from * around, ch 3, join to 3rd ch of first ch 6. Fasten off.

Explanation: Make sure that you know how to do cluster stitches. Review material on page 91. The chain one to secure the cluster is not counted as the first chain of the next chain four. (See photograph.)

JOINING MEDALLIONS

Medallions may be joined in numerous ways. Select a method you wish to use. The medallions must be finished and the ends worked in. Then they can be joined with a row of connecting crochet, using a variety of different stitches in the same color or in a contrasting color. The finished medallions can be sewed together, or they may be put together using a slip stitch. Another nice method to use is, a joining on the last row of each medallion, if the last row lends itself to an attractive joining. As stated before, the roll stitch medallion may be joined at the picots, and any other medallion which has picots on the last row can be joined in the same way.

Example of Joining With Fancy Edging

The hexagonal medallion on page 257 is used for the example joining. Join a contrasting colored yarn in the treble crochet stitch at the point of one side of the first medallion and work completely around the medallion as follows: Chain three, in the same treble crochet stitch work (one double crochet stitch, chain three, two double crochet stitches); * skip the next double crochet stitch in the previous round, place one single crochet stitch in the next double crochet stitch, chain five, skip two double crochet stitches, one single crochet stitch in the next double crochet stitch. Skip the next double crochet stitch, work a corner in the next treble crochet stitch (two double crochet stitches, chain three, two double crochet stitches); repeat from * around. After the last corner has been made (the sixth corner), one side is left unworked. Work along that side as follows: Skip the next double crochet stitch, place one single crochet stitch in the next double crochet stitch, chain five, skip two double crochet stitches, one single crochet stitch in the next double crochet stitch; you are now back to the starting place. Join with a slip stitch to the top of the turning chain and fasten off.

Start the edging on the second medallion by joining the contrasting colored yarn in the treble crochet stitch at the point of one side, as was just explained for edging the first medallion.

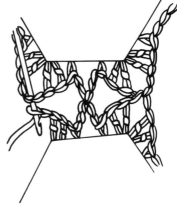

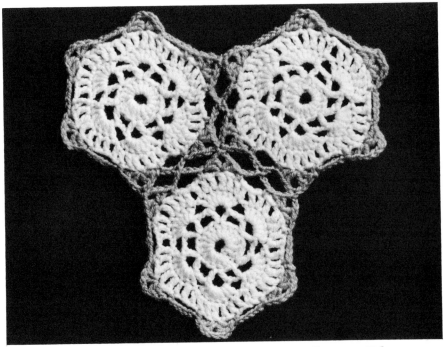

Three Hexagon Medallions Joined with Fancy Edge

Work as before across one side until you come to the treble crochet stitch at the next corner. Then work two double crochet
stitches in the treble crochet stitch, chain two, remove the hook
from the loop, insert the hook into the center chain of the chain
three at the point of the first medallion *and also through the loop
which was on the hook*, and pull the loop through, chain one,
two double crochet stitches in the same treble crochet stitch of
the second medallion, skip one double crochet stitch, single crochet stitch in the next double crochet stitch, chain three, remove the hook from the loop, insert the hook into the center
chain (of the chain five of the first medallion) *and also into the
loop which was on the hook*, and pull the loop through, chain two,
skip the next two double crochet stitches, and single crochet in
the next double crochet stitch. Work the half corner of two

double crochet stitches in the corner treble crochet stitch, chain two, join to the next corner of the first medallion as just explained. One side has been joined. Now finish the round of the second medallion and fasten off.

See photograph of how the medallions are to be joined after the initial row of medallions. Notice that on six-sided medallions, the second row of medallions is staggered. You will not need to work half medallions if you are making a shell, but if you are making a cardigan, half medallions will need to be worked on the front edges, and perhaps at the armhole or neck shaping. See page 265 for instructions on how to make half medallions.

Joining by Slip Stitching

The slip stitching method of joining applies to square-shaped medallions with straight-line edges. Complete all medallions and fasten ends. With the right sides of the two medallions to be joined facing each other, join matching yarn at one corner and slip stitch the edges together, matching stitch for stitch, and place the hook through the back loops of each medallion. (See drawing.)

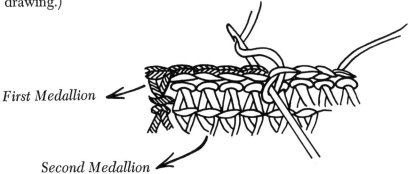

First Medallion

Second Medallion

Joining by Sewing

The sewing method of joining applies to square or hexagonal medallions with straight-line edges. Complete all medallions and

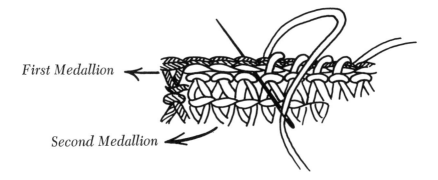

First Medallion ←

Second Medallion ←

work in all ends. With the right sides of the two medallions together, attach the yarn at one corner and sew the medallions together, matching stitch for stitch, placing the needle through the back loops of each stitch. (See drawing.)

Joining at Picots

Complete the first medallion, fasten off the yarn, and work in the ends. Work the second medallion to the last row. When working the last row on the second medallion, work to the first picot you wish to join. Place the two medallions side by side, work to the *center* chain stitch of the picot (if the picot consists of three chains, work *two* chains before joining), remove the hook from the loop; then place the hook in the *center* stitch of the picot to be joined on the first medallion. Place the hook back into the dropped loop and pull the loop through, chain one stitch, and finish the picot on the second medallion. Work along on the second medallion until the next joining picot; then join as just stated. (See drawing.)

WORKING HALF MEDALLIONS

It may be necessary to work half medallions (or partial medallions) for certain types of garments. These medallions are usually needed at neck shapings or around armholes.

Start the center of the medallion as you did previously. Work just half of the first round; then break off the yarn. Start the second round where the first round was started; work just half the round again. Do this with all rounds. You will have many ends to work in when the half medallion is finished. But there is no other way they can be worked since you cannot turn and work back over the row from the other direction. If you should do so, the *wrong* side would be showing on every other row, and this would be very noticeable. One-fourth and three-fourths medallions are worked in the same manner.

OTHER METHODS OF STARTING MEDALLIONS

Not all medallions are started in the center by working a chain of a specified number of stitches.

A hard core center may be made by winding the yarn around your index finger several times; then the first row of single crochet stitches (or any other stitch) is placed through the entire ring. (See drawing.)

You may wish to make a very tight center; chain two stitches, place six single crochet stitches in the second chain from the hook, and join with a slip stitch. (See drawing.)

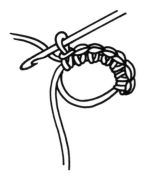

Another way to make a tight center is to wrap the yarn once around your index finger (leaving an end of approximately three inches). Work the specified number of single crochet stitches into the one-thread circle that you just made, and then join with a slip stitch. Tighten the center thread by pulling tightly on the three-inch end.

DIAGRAMS FOR MEDALLION GARMENTS

Square medallions are easier to gauge into the diagram than round, hexagonal, or octagonal medallions; therefore, it is best to make your first garment using a square medallion pattern. Select a garment with simple lines and without sleeves, such as a vest or a plain skirt. After the fitting technique has been mastered, there is no limit to the type of garments you will be able to make.

If you can obtain Japanese pattern books, the layouts are figured for you; then you need only adjust their layouts to your own measurements. There are more medallion patterns becoming available in the American pattern books.

Example Diagram

Select a medallion pattern, suitable yarn and hook, and make up several medallions. Block them and join them together. Take the measurement of at least two medallions, including the joinings. Next, proceed to take your measurements for a vest which just comes together in the front (no overlap). You will need to allow approximately two inches more than your bust measurement. For example, if your bust measurement is thirty-four inches, your crochet measurement should be thirty-six inches. Half of the bust measurement should be taken for the back piece (eighteen inches) and nine inches for each front. Study Drawing 1,

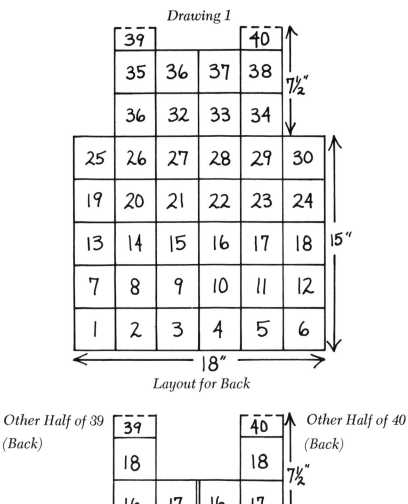

Drawing 1

Layout for Back

Other Half of 39
(Back)

Other Half of 40
(Back)

Layout for Front

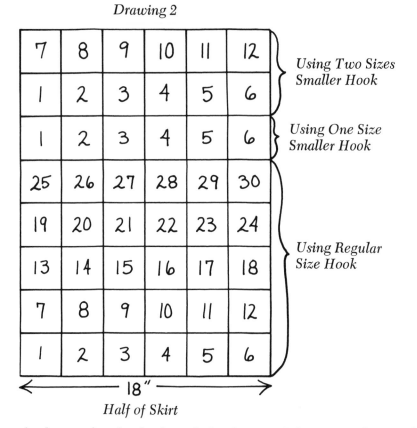

Drawing 2

7	8	9	10	11	12
1	2	3	4	5	6
1	2	3	4	5	6
25	26	27	28	29	30
19	20	21	22	23	24
13	14	15	16	17	18
7	8	9	10	11	12
1	2	3	4	5	6

Using Two Sizes Smaller Hook

Using One Size Smaller Hook

Using Regular Size Hook

← 18" →

Half of Skirt

the layout for the back and the fronts of the vest. Three-inch joined medallions are used. Notice that the armhole depth used in the example is seven and one-half inches.

Study Drawing 2, which shows half of the skirt using the same three-inch, joined medallions. This skirt has a row of six medallions at the bottom edge of the front and six medallions at the bottom edge of the back (twelve medallions in all). Since a skirt should taper in for the waistline (unless you want it gathered), hook sizes were changed on the sixth row to one size smaller and on the seventh and eighth rows the hook size was changed to two sizes smaller. By using smaller hooks, the medallions will be smaller and this proecdure gives the necessary shaping at the waist.

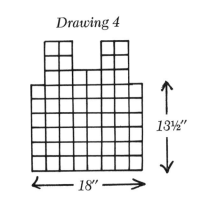

Drawing 4

13½″

18″

Shell with Square Medallions

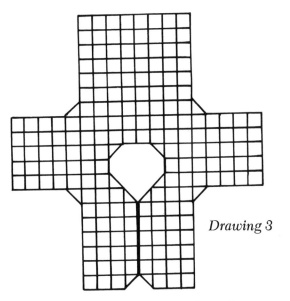

Drawing 3

Medallions Approximately 2¼″

Drawing 3 shows the layout for a simple-line jacket with sleeves made of square medallions.

A certain amount of experimenting may be necessary in order to get the correct start. If the joined medallions you made do not quite fit the space (according to your measurements), make several new ones, using larger or smaller hooks, until the desired inch measurement is obtained. If you desire, wider or narrower joinings may be used. This will change the overall inch measurements to fit the requirements. Such experimenting will be necessary for any shaped medallion. Make up several medallions, join them, and see how close they come to the needed measurements.

Drawings 4–10 show a variety of ideas for garments that can be made with medallions. The eight-sided medallion should be treated like the square or the diamond medallion. Some of these layouts require half or partial medallions.

Note: Curved edges at necklines or armholes may be formed by fill-in stitches on the joining rows, or final trimming rows may

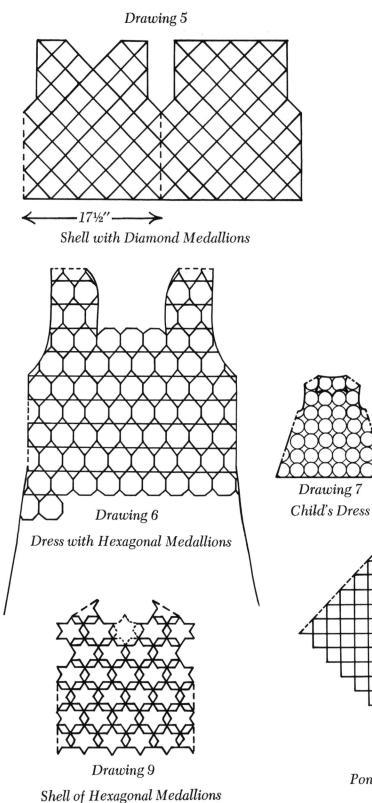

Drawing 5

← 17½″ →

Shell with Diamond Medallions

Drawing 6

Dress with Hexagonal Medallions

Drawing 7

Child's Dress

Drawing 8

Layout Suitable for
Open or Closed Ves
Tunic Top
Dress, or Shell

Drawing 9

Shell of Hexagonal Medallions

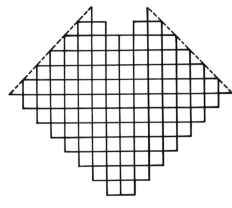

Drawing 10

Poncho with Square

be added to the front edges, neck, and armhole edges. At this time, straight edges may be made into curved edges by making shorter or longer stitches at the point you want to curve. See the drawing (page 284) in the collection of medallions using Japanese symbols.

UNDERSTANDING JAPANESE SYMBOLS

Each Japanese symbol represents a certain type crochet stitch. A key to reading the symbols is given in the pattern book, with a drawing of each stitch. (See drawing.)

It is much easier to work a design from symbols than to read instructions in words in pattern books. At a glance one can tell what kind of stitch is used and exactly where it is placed. One can see how many shells, popcorns, etc. are grouped together and what comes between them. One can also tell what the finished medallion or pattern will look like.

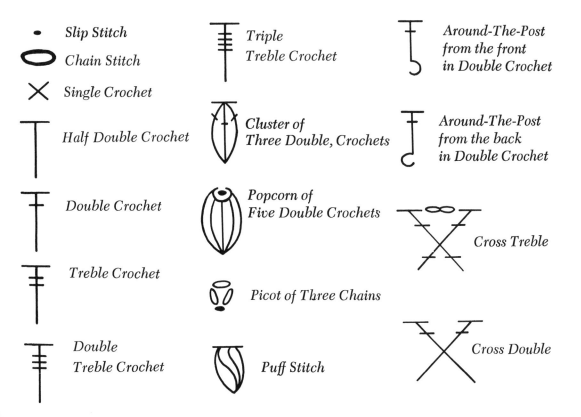

Example Diagrams in Japanese Symbols

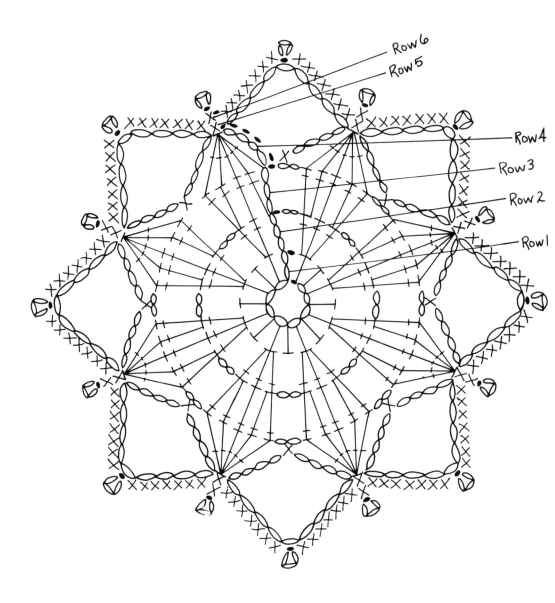

Wildflower Medallion

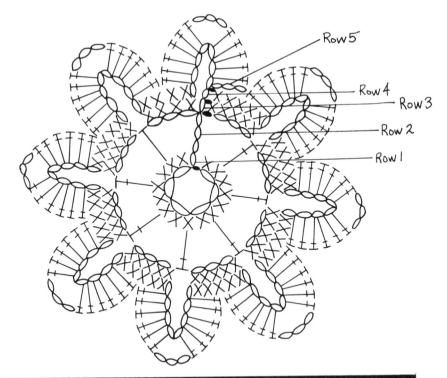

Row 5

Row 4

Row 3

Row 2

Row 1

Sunflower Medallion

Flower Box Medallion

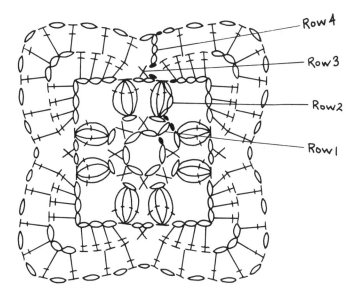

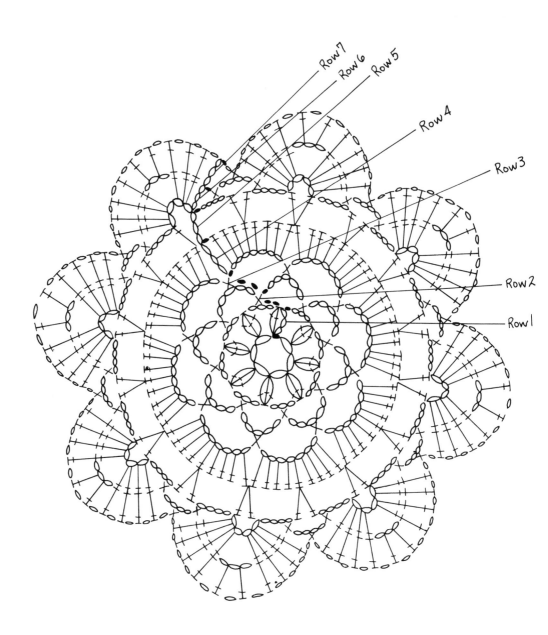

Row7
Row6
Row5
Row4
Row3
Row2
Row1

Snowflake Medallion

Crown Medallion

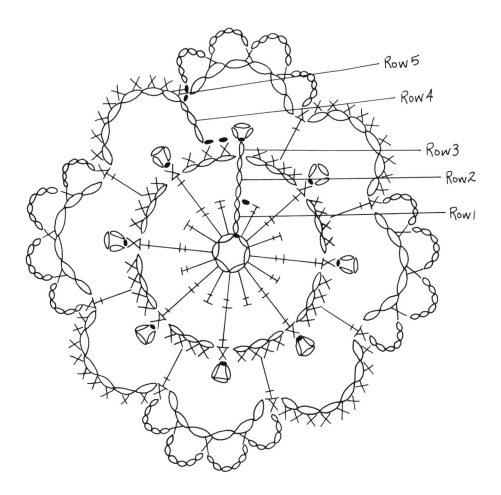

Row 5
Row 4
Row 3
Row 2
Row 1

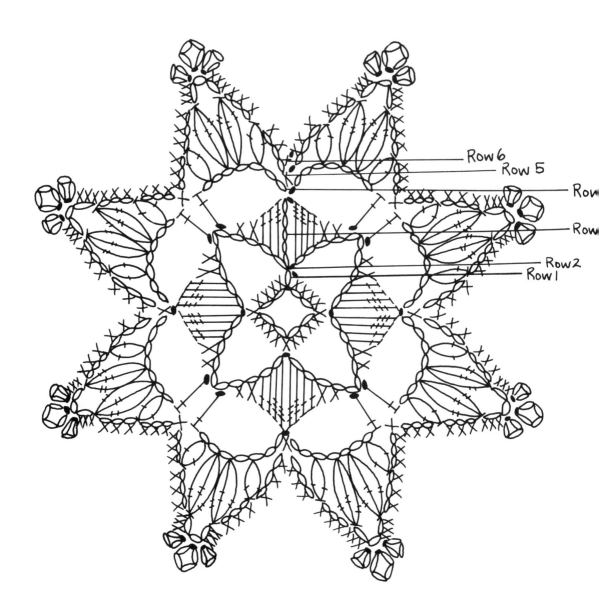

Row 6
Row 5
Row
Row
Row 2
Row 1

Starflower Medallion

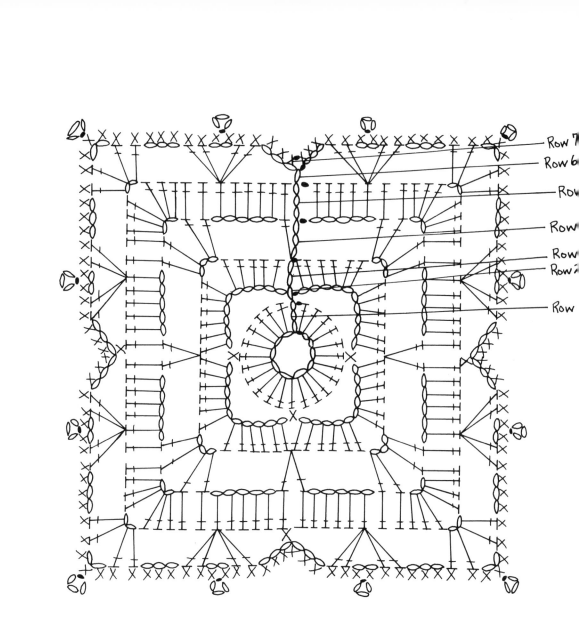

Row 7
Row 6
Row
Row
Row
Row 2
Row

Square-on-Square Medallion

OTHER USES FOR MEDALLIONS

Combining Medallions with Fabrics

If you are handy with the needle and sewing machine, and are
accustomed to sewing many of your own garments, dainty crochet
medallions may be used in conjunction with home sewing to
make lovely original designs. They may be used as a yoke, in-
sertions, borders, pockets, collars, complete sleeves, and in many
other ways.

Medallions look especially pretty applied on lightweight woolen
fabrics of the same color. A contrasting color may also be used.
After the design has been decided upon and the medallions have
been worked, blocked, and joined together, carefully tack them
to the woolen fabric with sewing thread. Trim away the fabric
underneath the medallions, and with very small stitches over-
cast the cut edges.

See the following layout suggestions using various types of
medallions.

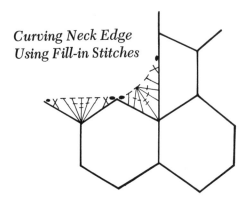

*Curving Neck Edge
Using Fill-in Stitches*

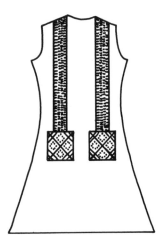

Note: The pretty pocket worked in popcorn stitch came from a very old crochet bedspread pattern. The strip of double crochet, approximately two inches wide, runs from the shoulder seam to just below the pocket opening. The instructions for the pocket square are as follows:

Ch 5, join with a sl st to form ring.

Rnd 1: Ch 3 (to count as dc at beg of each rnd), 2 dc in ring, * ch 3, 3 dc in ring, repeat from * 2 more times, ch 3, join with sl st to 3rd st of ch 3 first made. Join each rnd in this way.

Rnd 2: Ch 3, dc in next 2 dc (picking up back lp only throughout), 2 dc in sp, * ch 3, 2 dc in sp, dc in each of next 3 dc, 2 dc in next sp, repeat from * around, ending with ch 3, 2 dc in sp, and join with sl st as before.

Rnd 3: Ch 3, 1 pc in next dc (to make pc work 5 dc in next st, drop lp from hook, insert hook through top of 1st dc, pick up dropped lp and draw loop through, ch 1 to secure popcorn), dc in each of next 3 dc, 2 dc in next sp, * ch 3, 2 dc in same sp, dc in each of next 3 dc, 1 pc in next dc, dc in each of next 3 dc, 2 dc in next sp, repeat from * around, ending with dc in each of next 2 dc, join with sl st as before.

Rnd 4: Ch 3, * dc in next pc, dc in next dc, 1 pc in next dc, dc in each of next 3 dc, 2 dc in sp, ch 3, 2 dc in same sp, dc in each of next 3 dc, 1 pc in next dc, 1 dc in next dc, repeat from * around, join.

Rnd 5: Ch 3, * 1 pc in next dc, dc in each of next 3 dc, 1 pc in next dc, dc in each of next 3 dc, 2 dc in sp, ch 3, 2 dc in same sp, dc in each of next 3 dc, 1 pc in next dc, dc in each of next 3 dc, repeat from * around, join.

Rnds 6 and 7: Work in same manner, having 4 pc sts in a section in the 6th rnd and 5 pc sts in a section in the 7th rnd.

Rnd 8: Work same as before, placing (2dc, ch 3, 2 dc) in each corner and working only 4 pc sts in a section as on the 6th rnd.

Rnd 9: Work as before, adding corner sts but placing only 3 pc sts in each section.

Rnds 10 and 11: Continue increasing at corners as before, and placing 2 pc sts in each section on rnd 10, and only 1 pc st in rnd 11.

Rnd 12: Work around in dc throughout each section with no pc sts and increasing as before at each corner.

Work one row of reverse crochet in each stitch around (see page 294). Fasten off.

Square Pocket Medallion—Popcorn Stitch

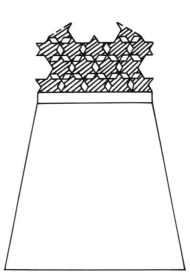

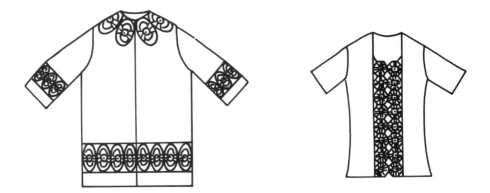

Rugs

Why not try your luck using medallions for making bathroom rugs or small scatter rugs? There are many medallions available which would lend themselves nicely to rug-making. Choose a

Hexagon Medallion for Rug

medallion that is not too lacy. Join the hexagonal, square or round medallions for the desired shape and size, and fringe them if you wish. See the photographs and the instructions for two medallions suitable for rugs.

HEXAGONAL MEDALLION RUG

Rnd 1: Ch 3, 14 dc in 1st st; join with a sl st.

Rnd 2: Ch 3, 1 dc in same st, 2 dc in each dc around (30 dc), join with a sl st to top of 1st ch 3.

Rnd 3: Ch 3, 2 dc in next dc, 1 dc in next dc, 2 dc in next dc, 1 dc in next dc (7 dc in all counting ch 3 as 1 dc), * ch 1, 7 dc in next 5 dc as before; repeat from * around ending ch 1, join to top of beg ch 3 (6 ch-1 spaces).

Rnd 4: Ch 3, dc in each of next 2 dc, popcorn in next dc (to make popcorn work 5 dc in next dc; remove hook from loop, insert hook in 1st dc and also in dropped loop, pull loop through, ch 1 to secure popcorn), 1 dc in each of next 3 dc, ch 2, * dc in each of next 3 dc, popcorn in next dc, dc in each of next 3 dc, ch 2; repeat from * around, join with sl st to 3rd st of beg ch 3.

Rnd 5: Ch 3, dc in last ch-2 sp, 2 dc in next dc, 1 dc in next dc, 2 dc in pc, 1 dc in next dc, 2 dc in next dc, 1 dc in next dc, 1 dc in next sp (12 dc on one side). * Ch 2, 1 dc in same sp, 1 dc in next dc, 2 dc in next dc, 1 dc in next dc, 2 dc in pc, 1 dc in next dc, 2 dc in next dc, 1 dc in next dc, 1 dc in next sp; repeat from * ending ch 2, join with sl st to 3rd ch of beg ch 3.

Rnd 6: Ch 3, 1 dc in next dc, 1 dc in next dc, pc in next dc, 1 dc in each of next 4 dc, pc in next dc, 1 dc in each of next 3 dc, * ch 2, 1 dc in next 3 dc, pc in next dc, 1 dc in each of next 4 dc, pc in next dc, 1 dc in next 3 dc; repeat from * end ch 2, join with sl st to top of beg ch 3. Fasten off.

SQUARE MEDALLION RUG

Ch 4, join with sl st.

Rnd 1: Ch 3 (to count as 1 dc), 2 dc in ring, * ch 2, 3 dc in ring; repeat from * 2 times, end ch 2, join to top of beg ch 3 (4 ch-2 corners).

Rnd 2: Ch 3 (to count as 1 dc), 1 dc in corner (to the right), * 1 dc in next dc, ch 1, skip 1 dc, dc in next dc; in ch-2 corner make (2 dc, ch 2, 2 dc); repeat from * end last repeat 2 dc, ch 2, join with sl st to beg ch-3. (Start and end all rnds as before, working 2 dc, ch 2, 2 dc in each corner.)

Rnd 3: Ch 3, 1 dc in corner, 1 dc in each of next 3 dc, ch 1, 1 dc in each of next 3 dc, 2 dc in ch-2 sp, ch 2. One side of square completed. Continue around other 3 sides in same manner; join as before.

Rnd 4: Ch 3, 1 dc in corner, 1 dc in each of next 5 dc, ch 1, dc in each of next 5 dc, 2 dc in ch-2 sp (corner), ch 2. One side of square completed. Continue around other 3 sides in same manner; join as before.

Rnd 5: Ch 3, 1 dc in corner, 1 dc in each of next 7 dc, ch 1, 1 dc in each of next 7 dc, 2 dc in ch-2 sp (corner), ch 2. One side of square completed. Continue around other 3 sides in same manner; join as before.

Rnd 6: Ch 3, 1 dc in corner, 1 dc in each of next 7 dc, ch 1, sk 1 dc, dc in next dc, 1 dc in ch-1 sp, 1 dc in next dc, ch 1, sk 1 dc, dc in each of next 7 dc, 2 dc in corner, ch 2. One side of square completed. Continue around other 3 sides in same manner; join as before.

Rnd 7: Ch 3, 1 dc in corner, 1 dc in each of next 7 dc, ch 1, sk 1 dc, 1 dc in next dc, 1 dc in ch-1 sp, 1 dc in next dc, ch 1, sk 1 dc, 1 dc in next dc, 1 dc in ch-1 sp, 1 dc in next dc, ch 1, sk 1 dc, 1 dc in each of next 7 dc, 2 dc in ch-2 (corner), ch 2. One side of square completed. Continue around other 3 sides in same manner; join as before. Fasten off.

Wall Hangings and Pictures

You might be interested in making some decorative items for your home. A string of joined medallions would make a beautiful wall hanging. Or, make a unique picture using a large lacy medallion. Use very fine crochet threads. Block it and mount it on polished wood and frame it for a conversation piece. You will be surprised at how handsome a design of this kind will look against a dark, interestingly grained wood. From a distance, one can see the dainty design of light threads against the background, and as one comes closer to the picture, the lovely stitches stand out in third dimension.

14 Trims and Edgings

Edgings
    Reverse crochet
    Mile-a-minute
    Popcorn
    Floweret

Tassels

Buttons
    Crocheted buttons on curtain rings
    Crocheted button balls

Fringe
    Simple knotted fringe
    Double knotted fringe

14   Trims and Edgings

Edgings and trims to finish garments are usually given with the pattern. Or you may wish to try out some of the suggestions that follow.

EDGINGS

Reverse Crochet

A very suitable edging is reverse crochet. It is quite plain, or tailored, and applies nicely to most any type garment that does not require a lacy edging.

After the first establishing row of single crochet stitches has been placed on the garment, do not fasten off the yarn. Chain one stitch, and do *not* turn the work around. Then, place a row of single crochet stitches, working in the opposite direction (from left to right). See drawing. A row of backward double crochet stitches may be used if you wish this last row to be deeper.

Reverse Crochet

Mile-A-Minute Edge

Mile-a-Minute

The so-called mile-a-minute edging has been used by many generations of crocheters. This deep lacy edging consists of only one row; consequently, the crocheter can do the edging approximately a mile in one minute (almost)!

After one row of establishing single crochet stitches has been placed on the edge of the garment, work the mile-a-minute as follows: Chain seven, place one double crochet stitch in the fourth chain from the hook, then place one double crochet stitch in the *same* single crochet stitch where the chain seven began, * skip three single crochet stitches, double crochet in the next single crochet stitch, chain four, double crochet in the fourth chain from the hook, double crochet in the same single crochet stitch where the chain four began. Repeat from the *.

Popcorn

This is another popular old edging. Work one row of establishing single crochet stitches and fasten off. With the right side of the work facing you, attach the yarn at the same end where the first establishing row began. Single crochet in the next five single crochet stitches (in the establishing row); chain three, work a popcorn stitch consisting of five double crochet stitches in the third chain of the chain three just worked. Remove the hook from the loop insert the hook into the top of the first double crochet stitch, pick up the dropped loop and pull the loop through. Then, chain one stitch to secure the popcorn, chain three, slip stitch into the top of the single crochet stitch at the base of the popcorn. Single crochet in the next five stitches; repeat from the * across the row.

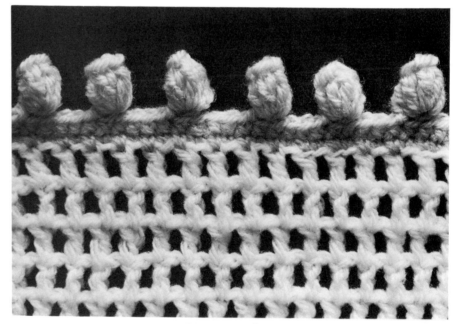

Popcorn Edge

Floweret

This pretty little edge would be suitable for trimming baby garments, little girl's dresses, caps, etc. Or it would add a delicate touch around the neck and armholes of lacy shells and blouses. This is another very old pattern found in a crochet booklet dated 1890. The instructions were so poorly written, it was necessary to rewrite them by looking at a picture of the edging and a little experimentation.

Ch 6, join with a sl st to form ring; ch 1, 1 sc in ring, * ch 4, 2 trc cluster in ring (to make cluster, work 2 trc in ring and hold back last lp on each trc, yo and pull through 3 lps on hook), ch 4, sc in ring, repeat from * 4 times more (5 petals of flower), ch 16, sl st in 6th ch from hook (to form another ring), ch 1, 1 sc in ring, repeat between * for another floweret. Continue to form more flowerets from the ch 16 for desired length.

Note: Each new floweret starts at the chain sixteen. (See photograph.)

Floweret Edge

TASSELS

Make a pretty tassel using the following instructions:

Wind yarn around a 3″ cardboard 20 times. Tie securely at one end of wraps, leaving 3″ ends, then cut at the other end. With another piece of yarn, wrap around tassel approximately ¾″ from tied end 5 times (tightly). Then crochet through the wrappings 7 sc around. Make 4 more rounds without joining, or 35 sts in all, sl st in every other stitch to close off. Fasten off and work in end.

Tassel

BUTTONS

Crocheted Buttons on Curtain Rings

Tailored buttons may be made over plastic curtain rings. Make a slip knot in the yarn; then work single crochet stitches into the ring, counting the stitches until you have completely filled the ring. Make a note of the number of stitches you worked. Cut off the yarn, leaving approximately twelve inches. Thread the yarn into a tapestry needle and take the needle through the back of every other stitch completely around the ring, drawing up on the yarn tightly so that the edge draws in to form the inside of the bottom. Take several stitches to secure, and then, with the yarn that is left, sew the button onto the garment with an "×" stitch through the center of the button. When making additional buttons, use the same number of single crochet stitches so that all of the buttons will be uniform.

Crocheted Button Balls

Use the following instructions to make crocheted buttons:

Chain four and join with slip stitch to form a ring.

Round 1: Six single crochet stitches in ring. Do not join at end of rounds.

Round 2: Two single crochet stitches in each single crochet stitch (twelve single crochet stitches).

Round 3: * Two single crochet stitches in one single crochet stitch, one single crochet stitch in next crochet stitch; repeat from * around (eighteen single crochet stitches).

Round 4: (decrease round): Single crochet in every other single crochet stitch (nine single crochet sttiches). At this point, stuff the button with cotton—as much as it will hold.

Finishing rounds: One single crochet stitch in every other single crochet stitch until no stitches remain.

Sew on the button ball with the remaining yarn.

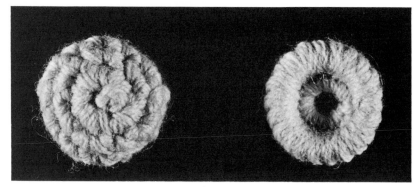

Two Crocheted Buttons

FRINGE

Simple Knotted Fringe

Decide upon the length of fringe you wish to use and the number of strands. Fold the fringe in half, and from the *wrong* side of the garment, insert the crochet hook though the stitch and pull the folded loop through; then bring both ends through the loop and tighten to form a knot. The knot will be formed on the *right* side of the work. (See drawing.)

 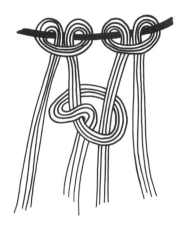

Double Knotted Fringe

First work simple knotted fringe along the entire edge. To work the double knotted fringe, take the right half of the first fringe and join it to the left half of the second fringe. Wrap the #1 strand around the #2 strand; then, pull the loose end of the #1 fringe through that circle and tighten the loop by pulling down.

The second row should start approximately one inch below the first row of single knots. Trim the ends of the fringe evenly.

Double Knotted Fringe

Index